VEGETARIAN
ANY DAY

VEGETARIAN
ANY DAY

OVER 100 SIMPLE, HEALTHY, SATISFYING MEATLESS RECIPES

PATRICIA GREEN &
CAROLYN HEMMING

PENGUIN

an imprint of Penguin Canada, a division of Penguin Random House Canada Limited

Canada • USA • UK • Ireland • Australia • New Zealand • India • South Africa • China

First published 2017

www.penguinrandomhouse.ca

LIBRARY AND ARCHIVES CANADA CATALOGUING IN PUBLICATION

Green, Patricia, author
    Vegetarian any day : over 100 simple, healthy, satisfying meatless recipes /
Patricia Green and Carolyn Hemming.

Includes index.
ISBN 978-0-14-319049-3 (paperback)
ISBN 978-0-7352-3296-9 (electronic)

    1. Vegetarian cooking. 2. Cookbooks. I. Hemming, Carolyn, author II. Title.

TX837.G74 2017   641.5'636   C2016-906078-0

Book design by Leah Springate
Cover images by Ryan Szulc
Food photography by Ryan Szulc
Food styling by Nancy Midwicki
Prop styling by Patricia Green, Carolyn Hemming, Ryan Szulc, and Nancy Midwicki

Printed and bound in China

10 9 8 7 6 5 4 3 2 1

ALSO BY PATRICIA GREEN
AND CAROLYN HEMMING

Sweet Goodness
Grain Power
Quinoa Revolution
Quinoa 365

CONTENTS

INTRODUCTION

EATING LESS MEAT

Are you a flexitarian? We asked our dry-cleaner, dentist, school principal, mail carrier, lawyer, flight attendant, pharmacist, grocery store cashier, neighbours and even our tax planner, Gary, who admitted, he too, eats meatless a couple of times a week. It was interesting to discover that for many, eating meatless *occasionally* is becoming a choice—though not necessarily a *conscious* one. Flexitarian is the recently coined term to identify people who occasionally eat meatless. So you may already be flexitarian, and you don't even know it. Adding a few new vegetarian recipes to your cooking routine will make it even easier to eat meatless, be healthful and enjoy a long list of nutritional benefits.

The concept of Meatless Mondays has recently raised awareness of eating vegetarian once a week. It may come from ethical, social or political convictions. Maybe it's the pursuit of improved health and longevity, or quite possibly it is simply a circumstance of gradually changing habits. It's not rocket science, you may say; eating habits evolve. But did we ever expect that surrounded by an abundance of cross-cultural meat options from alligator chorizo to venison meatloaf, that our human, omnivorous, once hunter-gatherer selves would maybe one day choose a dish, say, *sans* meat? With meat being such a staple part of the traditional North American diet and a burger joint on every major thoroughfare, it may have seemed doubtful

that day would ever come. But thanks to good ol' mom and those seaweed chips she kept in the cupboard, Patricia and I both have always been fairly open to evolving food habits.

While Patricia was always somewhat cooperative in sampling mom's uber-healthful cooking, I was more reluctant and skeptical, especially when it came to eating meat. I recall sitting at the dinner table for hours in protest, long after the dishes were cleared and washed, firmly committed to resisting clam chowder or mom's favourite mineral supplement, liver. I can still see my Viking father towering over me, quizzically asking how I could possibly refuse to eat what he saw as one of the most beloved foods of my '70s childhood, the cheeseburger. The texture and flavour just didn't appeal to me.

Nowadays, we all have a new label depending on our eating habits. I've never strayed from being a picky and occasional meat-eater, making me a veteran flexitarian. Patricia has gone from flexitarian to committed pescetarian (a vegetarian who eats fish), as that is what most agrees with her stomach. And our once-upon-a-time, daily-meat-loving husbands now realize they've been flexitarians . . . for years!

In 2010, after the incredible success of our first book, *Quinoa 365: The Everyday Superfood*, we were invited to speak to the employees of a large, national meat processor. With a plethora of protein-rich recipes under our belts, many of which offered meat alternatives, we asked the lead scientist, "Why us?" To our fascination, she replied, "Meat is no longer the main dish; it's the side." It's true, red meat consumption has been decreasing in Canada and the United States since the late '90s as a result of rising costs, changing palates, an aging population, ethical or environmental concerns, religious practice and a shift to overall healthier lifestyles.

We can't ignore that "to eat or not to eat meat" is a debate that continues to be a contentious issue. Ethical and political arguments for eating meatless raise obvious concerns about animal cruelty and environmental destruction, offering strong support for vegetarian lifestyles. Eating meat has also been linked to disease; however, science reveals that the correlation may arise from overconsumption, rather than average consumption. Eating meat can be an easy way to get a rich dose of protein and nutrients, but it may be wise to reduce the amount we consume, even if health is our only reason. The current recommendation for healthy meat consumption is no more than one serving of meat three times a week. Even our favourite global food expert, Michael Pollan, in his *New York Times* bestseller *In Defense of Food*, claims although he hasn't found a compelling enough reason to exclude meat completely from his diet, he definitely agrees with reducing the amount of it in your diet.

Medical research has also shown that increased fruit and vegetable intake can boost your health and provide benefits that include improved immune function and a reduced risk of cardiovascular disease, high blood pressure, type 2 diabetes, cancer and even allergies. But if you plan to eliminate meat from your diet, you must ensure your body is nourished with its required protein and nutrients. Being a full-time vegetarian demands a bit of effort to make sure you're eating what you need to prevent serious illness. Avoiding meat for health reasons can end up doing more harm than good if you aren't receiving the vitamins and minerals your body needs to stay healthy.

As the food landscape quickly changes and our eating habits adjust, new companies are popping up all the time and offering new meat-alternative products and replacements for foods like eggs and mayonnaise. These products are made from plant-based ingredients such as soy, grains, seeds, and legumes, and some companies are experimenting with protein and mineral-rich algae and even insects. It's important, however, to be vigilant as new vegetarian products continue to flood the market. Choose healthful, whole foods over refined, and educate yourself about your choices by scrutinizing processing practices, additives, fillers and origins. In the words of Michael Pollan, whatever you're eating, just make sure it's "real food," not something manufactured in a lab.

Vegetarian cooking is anything but boring. If you are at all daunted by integrating vegetarian recipes into your repertoire, don't worry; there's nothing to fear. Vegetarian cooking is extremely easy and many simple recipes are suited to beginner cooks—and even better, these meatless meals are incredibly satisfying. It's not just big, leafy salads. Instead, think savoury vegetable lasagna, hearty risotto or a thick, juicy grilled mushroom burger worth every bite. You may notice the flavour of meatless dishes is amplified when you use local produce that is in season. Cooking with seasonal fruits and vegetables from your own neck of the woods has many benefits. The most obvious is that it's less costly—growing and shipping from elsewhere generally means a higher price tag. Imported produce has also likely endured necessary "special care," such as premature harvesting, unnatural chilling and prolonged storage. Try incorporating vegetables and fruits from your local markets and independent farmers, and you'll notice how it elevates taste and quality.

At certain times of the year, eating strictly seasonally and locally is much more difficult, if not almost impossible. So explore the selection of unusual, fresh, whole foods available in mainstream grocery stores. Once considered a tiresome household chore, food prep is now all the rage, and the kitchen is vying for top spot as sexiest room in the house. In one quick walk through any produce aisle, you can discover foods like mini turnips, French baby carrots, a wide selection of unusual mushrooms, kale blossoms and tiny, exotic radishes bursting with colour. People are experimenting with different culinary fads, including cooking with live cultures and fermented products, pickling and preserving, and exploring sour and bitter foods and clashing flavour combinations, such as sweet and salty or spicy and smoked. We are undoubtedly in the midst of a food renaissance, with eating and cooking becoming increasingly important daily experiences. Look around and you'll discover an abundance of exciting foods with which to create new and delicious recipes in your kitchen.

Eating meatless just one or even a few days a week is a simple lifestyle change that can enhance your health, but you don't necessarily need that reason to make the shift to the recipes in this book. Perhaps you are already a vegetarian or just want to eat great food and discover tasty alternatives to your usual rotation of recipes. We love that meatless food preparation forces you to expand your culinary creativity. The recipes in *Vegetarian Any Day* begin with the goal of being delicious. Sticking with our usual modus operandi, we have made these delectable dishes with easily accessible and nutritious ingredients and with that same anyone-can-cook attitude. We've created satisfying recipes that don't feel like they're missing anything; meals that will please, surprise and nourish.

Flexitarians, both new and experienced, can enjoy these delicious recipes, which will make you forget they happen to be vegetarian. So whether your version of meatless is a result of conscious choice or not, whatever day of the week you choose, bon appétit! (Or as we'd say in Norwegian, *vær så god!*)

Patricia and Carolyn

VEGETARIAN 101

Vegetarian cooking is simple and made easier if you have a few important staples on hand. The first trick is stocking your pantry with those meatless ingredients that you and your family prefer, whether beans or legumes, ancient grains, mushrooms or sweet potatoes (for a list of pantry items, see page 18). Your favourite vegetarian essentials are key for successful vegetarian recipe prep, as they'll provide the most meal possibilities. It's helpful to plan your recipes on the weekend and buy what you'll need before the week begins and becomes too hectic. Start with easy recipes that include ingredients you're familiar with so they don't feel too foreign and will ultimately be easier to adopt into your cooking routine. Be inspired and open-minded, and let your creative meatless cook emerge. Get a member (or two!) of your household involved as this will surely increase their chances of enjoying the meals too!

USING OIL IN RECIPES

Deciding which oil to use in a recipe can be confusing. Oil can be a healthier alternative to butter, since it contains more unsaturated, rather than saturated, fats. But how do you choose the healthiest oil that will also taste great?

Overall, vegetable oils used for cooking are generally healthy because they originate from plants. The healthiest of oils contain the most monounsaturated fats, are less refined and are higher in nutrients. These include virgin olive oil, peanut, canola, flaxseed, walnut, hemp, avocado and almond oils. Labels of "extra virgin" or "unrefined" means the oil is less processed and therefore contains even more nutrients.

An important factor in ensuring you are cooking oils in a healthy manner depends on whether or not the recipe requires heating your ingredients. High temperatures will cause the nutritional profile of oils to break down and change, becoming less healthy, so it is important to choose the appropriate oil for each application.

Oils that have a higher smoke point (temperature at which they burn) are the best for cooking at high temperatures. Grapeseed, camelina, vegetable, canola, corn, sunflower, safflower, peanut or a refined olive oil have a higher smoke point and are better for sautéing vegetables, such as onions or mushrooms, stir-frying, deep frying or using in any baked or cooked dishes. Recipes that do not require heat to prepare the dish, such as salads, dips and dressings, can use oils that are purer and less refined, including extra virgin olive oil, flaxseed, walnut and hemp oil.

INCORPORATING DRIED BEANS INTO YOUR COOKING

Preparing and rehydrating dried beans, instead of buying the canned variety, has great advantages.

First, dried beans are much less expensive. On average, one pound (half a kilogram) of dried beans is half the price of canned beans. Second, you might opt for dried beans if you're concerned about the additives. The canning process adds a lot of salt to properly preserve the beans, and although you can rinse much of it off when you drain the can, you can avoid it entirely by using dried beans. Third, many cans are still lined with Bisphenol A, more commonly referred to as BPA. Overexposure to BPA may be a health concern. Food manufacturers have been slow to change this, so if you can avoid canned goods, we recommend it.

Dried beans are full of nutrients and easy to simmer into soups, stews, casseroles and countless meatless meals. Black-eyed peas are easy to cook and in 45 to 50 minutes you can have delicious cooked beans, no soaking required. Lima beans or large white beans don't hold together well and tend to fall apart, so they are better for puréed soups, dips or sauces. We recommend cooking beans in larger batches and freezing them (for up to 3 months) for fast meal prep so you're never disappointed by forgetting to soak them!

How to Prepare Beans

Soaking dried beans for 24 hours or overnight will soften and prepare them for cooking. To soak, first clean and rinse the beans, then place them in a medium to large saucepan, depending on how much you are cooking. As a general rule, when soaking, the water to bean ratio is 3:1. Allow beans to soak overnight, then drain and rinse. Place a saucepan on the stovetop over medium-high heat and cook in 4 cups (1 L) of water for every 1 cup (250 mL) of beans. Bring to a boil and skim any film off the top. Reduce to a simmer and cook until the beans are tender, but not mushy (see the chart below for some general times). If desired, season with salt. Allow the beans to cool, then drain and rinse.

Bean Cooking Times

This chart shows the amount of time you need to cook various types of beans. It is based on 1 cup (250 mL) of beans (that have already been soaked overnight) or 1 cup (250 mL) of dry lentils cooked in 4 cups (1 L) of water. This will yield approximately 2 cups (500 mL) of either beans or lentils.

TYPE OF BEAN	TIME TO COOK (HOURS)
adzuki	1.25 to 1.5
black	1.5
black-eyed peas	1
fava	1.5 to 2
cannellini (white kidney)	1.5 to 2
chickpeas (garbanzo beans)	2 to 3
great northern	1.5 to 2
mung	0.75
navy	2.25
pinto	2 to 2.5
red	3
red kidney	1.5 to 2

HOW TO PREPARE DRIED MUSHROOMS

Using dried mushrooms is a great way to have a fresh mushroom taste without spending too much money or using the tasteless canned version. Dried mushrooms can be much less expensive than fresh ones, and you can combine flavours by mixing types. You might buy a small amount of expensive morels, for instance, and add them to other neutral-tasting dried mushrooms to get morel flavour without the high price of the fresh variety. Dried mushrooms are flavour-packed and take a small amount of time to rehydrate and use. Simply cover mushrooms with warm or room-temperature water and let sit for approximately 30 minutes. Mushrooms should be meaty and tender and ready for cooking. Hydrating water can be retained and used in soups, purées, sauces and more. Dried mushrooms can be found in most grocery stores in the international food aisles, and Asian grocers usually stock a large selection. Foraging for wild mushrooms is also becoming popular, with many people seeking to explore edible varieties available in their local forests. However, it's important to always use reference guides to ensure you identify non-poisonous varieties.

HOW TO USE MISO

Miso is a Japanese seasoning usually made of fermented soybeans (or other beans), rice, barley or any combination of them. It can provide an extra hit of savoury flavour, also referred to as "umami," to many recipes, especially meatless ones. The rich flavour of miso makes it a great addition to soups, dressings, sauces and marinades. We recommend you add miso as close to the end of the cooking process as possible to maintain its nutritional integrity.

Miso's fermented properties make it excellent for detox, and it has been known to restore health following illness, especially from radiation, chemotherapy or environmental chemical exposure. It has healthy binding agents that help to pull and eliminate toxins from the body. It is a complete protein, high in vitamin B and full of fermented enzymes that provide probiotics and aid digestion. It does have a strong flavour and can be high in sodium, but it is used only in small amounts to infuse a wonderfully savoury taste.

You can buy a few different types of miso. It is available at most major grocery stores in instant powder, freeze dried or paste forms and can come in a jar, in single-portion boxes or vacuum-packed. It can usually be found in the soup, organic or international food aisles and is especially easy to find at Asian markets and grocery stores. These are the most common types of miso:

- White Miso Made with fermented soybeans and rice, it is the lightest miso and also has the least amount of flavour and lowest sodium. Gluten-free brands are available.

- Yellow Miso A moderately flavoured version, it is slightly darker than white, but a nice choice if you want the most versatile option. It has been fermented longer than white miso and with a smaller amount of rice. Depending on the brand, it may contain more soybeans or barley. Gluten-free brands are available.

- Red Miso Fermented longer than other varieties, it has a darker appearance and stronger flavour. It has a higher salt content than the lighter versions and is made with a greater percentage of soybeans. Gluten-free brands are available.

- Barley Miso Slightly sweet, it is not as strong as pure soybean miso. It is not gluten-free.

- **Soybean Miso** Darker and usually less smooth, it doesn't contain any rice or barley but generally has a much stronger flavour. Gluten-free brands are available.

Generally, we use white, yellow or red miso. You can use any of these in our recipes if we do not specify. A good rule to remember is the darker the miso, the longer it has been fermented and as a result, the stronger the flavour. Since only small amounts of miso are usually used, if you're using a lighter version you may want to add a bit more and if a darker version, a bit less. To ensure you always end up with an even flavour profile, season your recipes as you go, to taste, and always store miso in the refrigerator. We prefer our miso to be organic, low sodium and MSG-free. There are also many gluten-free brands available.

TOFU BASICS

As tofu continues to increase in popularity, new varieties are constantly being introduced into the market. Made from the curds of coagulated soybean milk that is pressed into blocks, it is available in a range of firmness. We recommend using organic, non-GMO tofu whenever possible to avoid the toxic farming chemicals and genes modified inside the soybeans, as we don't yet know the effects of these substances on our bodies. Here's an outline of the most common types of tofu.

- **Soft** A custard-like tofu, it does not hold its shape well. It is great for desserts and in recipes where it can be blended into smoothies, dips and soups. It can be deep-fried but not without a batter to prevent excessive spitting from its high water content. Soft tofu varieties range from the softest, also known as silken, to extra-soft and soft.

- **Medium-Firm** This tofu is a balance between extra-firm and soft. It is still creamy but firm and can be used for dips, sauces, desserts and casseroles.

- **Pressed** Pressed tofu has the least amount of water content and can hold its shape while cooking. It can be shredded, cubed and baked.

- **Firm, Extra-Firm and Super-Firm** These types hold their shape well and increase in solidity from firm to super-firm. They can be easily cubed, sliced, baked, barbecued and stir-fried. These varieties are excellent choices for savoury dishes and work well added to salads. When pressed to remove water, they are also great in burgers as they soak up the flavours of marinades nicely.

- **Smoked** A solid tofu with a smoky flavour, this is a good option for the barbecue, in stir-fries and salads and for broiling.

THE TOFU ALTERNATIVE: TEXTURED VEGETABLE PROTEIN (TVP)

A common meat replacement, TVP is made from soy flour and is high in fibre, essential amino acids and minerals. It is dried and when prepared has a texture similar to ground meat. It can be bought as granules and chunks in a variety of flavours, but plain is the most widely sold. TVP just needs to be hydrated with water,

stock or sauce and is perfect for those who like its convenience. You can make it soft or chewy depending on the amount of liquid you use to hydrate it. It's inexpensive and, depending on storage, its shelf life can be a year or more. Be aware that it is a highly processed food, but if it's a product you like to use, we recommend always buying organic and MSG-free.

SALT: WHAT TO DO IN A PINCH

With so many salts available, how do you know which one to use? The truth is, you don't need much salt when cooking with fresh ingredients like vegetables and herbs. When you do need a dash, a very small amount goes a long way. Kosher salt is a popular choice. While it is coarser, it dissolves quickly. It is less dense than its finer-grained sibling, common table salt, so it offers greater control when salting recipes. Kosher salt is less processed and doesn't tend to have the added anti-caking agents regular table salt contains. Sea salt is also less processed and contains more trace minerals and retains a natural colour and flavour. A small pinch of sea salt can add a burst of flavour to just-cooked foods. Himalayan sea salt, like pink or black salts, are also less processed, may contain minerals and can even aid in proper nutrient absorption. Save your expensive, mineral-rich salts for finishing your dishes and use regular table salt for boiling water.

GROWING YOUR OWN SPROUTS AND MICROGREENS

Sprouting

Sprouting is a raw method of preparing your grains and seeds that can provide a living, nutrient-rich alternative to cooked foods.

Increasingly popular, sprouts are a great way to grow your own fresh food any time of the year, and you can't get any more local than your own kitchen! These foods are full of enzymes and rich in vitamins and minerals, and sprouting grains and seeds at home is incredibly simple.

When sprouting, it's best to use organic seeds and grains when possible, as they have been handled in a manner that reduces the risk of contamination, which is possible during this process. Quinoa is one of the quickest-sprouting seeds, however there is a wide array of home-grown sprouting options, including alfalfa, amaranth, adzuki bean, broccoli, buckwheat groats, chickpea, cress, fenugreek, green pea shoots, Kamut wheat, kañiwa, lentils, millet, mung bean, mustard seed, oats, onion, radish, sesame seed, snow peas, soybean, sunflower seed, teff, wheat berries and wild rice.

Sprouts are best eaten when they are small because they have more crunch and last longer. Sprouts that are larger and longer are softer in texture and deteriorate more quickly. Prepared sprouts should be stored in a glass container in the refrigerator with the lid open slightly to allow for air circulation. It is best to use them within 1 to 3 days of achieving the desired length. Be aware that they can develop an odour, slime or visible mould, which can result from a lack of air circulation, not enough rinsing or by sprouting in too warm an environment. If you see or smell any of these, discard the batch and try again. The final quantity of sprouts will depend on the amount of time the sprouts grow and their resulting length. Sprouts can be eaten as a nutritious snack on their own or used in salads, sandwiches, smoothies, stews, soups and casseroles.

Try using sprouts in the Vegetable Nori Wraps with Orange Ginger Miso Dressing (page 37) or to top the Blushing Beet and Blue Cheese Deviled Eggs with Toasted Pecans (page 43).

Sprouting Method

Wash your hands thoroughly. Place the sprouting seeds in a clean glass casserole dish (do not use plastic; it can have residual bacteria that may contaminate your sprouts). Pour in enough distilled water to cover the seeds, stir with a clean spoon and soak for the required time (see chart below) at room temperature for the first 4 hours and the remainder in a cool place.

Drain the water from the seeds by using a fine mesh strainer. While the seeds are in the strainer, rinse them with more distilled water. Rinse the casserole dish. Rinsing is important! It delivers critical moisture to the seeds so that they germinate. Return the drained and wet seeds to the casserole dish and cover, leaving a slight opening for air. Place in the refrigerator or a dark, cool location. Repeat the rinsing process every 8 to 10 hours until the seeds have sprouted to the desired length, at which time you can place them in indirect sunlight.

SPROUT SEEDS	SOAKING TIME (APPROXIMATE)
alfalfa	4 to 8 hours
amaranth	24 hours
beans	8 to 12 hours
buckwheat groats	use sprouting-grade seeds (found online or at specialty stores); follow package directions
chia	should be grown as microgreens, not as sprouts; soaking time is 1 hour in the cheesecloth; refer to page 13

SPROUT SEEDS	SOAKING TIME (APPROXIMATE)
green peas	8 to 10 hours
kañiwa	24 hours
lentils	12 hours
millet	use sprouting-grade seeds (found online or at specialty stores); follow package directions
mung beans	9 to 10 hours
oat groats	use sprouting-grade seeds (found online or at specialty stores); follow package directions
pumpkin seeds	6 to 8 hours
quinoa	1 to 4 hours
radish seeds	8 to 10 hours
sesame seeds	7 to 8 hours
sunflower seeds	7 to 8 hours
teff	1 to 4 hours
wheat berries	6 to 8 hours

Microgreens

Some grains and seeds need to be grown as microgreens rather than as sprouts. Sprouts are bunched together and soaked in water, but microgreens are grown vertically either in soil, on a felt pad or in some type of fabric. This is another great way to grow food in your own home regardless of where you live. They can be eaten in salads, such as the Microgreen and Fig Salad with Hemp Seed Gremolata (page 96), Lazy Layered Salad with Herbed Kefir Ranch Dressing (page 102), or add them to the Crisp Iceberg Wedge Salad with Cashews and Chili Mango Dressing (page 93), Orange and Beet Salad with Toasted Walnuts (page 101) and topping the Ginger Lime Edamame Noodle Bowl (page 170). Microgreens are also a delicious addition to sandwiches or smoothies, juiced, used as garnishes or even eaten alone. Some research suggests that eating these immature fresh microgreens has even more benefits than consuming them in their mature state, as young plants have been found to contain higher levels of enzymes and nutrients.

Most seeds and grains can be sown as microgreens. As with sprouts, millet, buckwheat and oats should be purchased specifically as sprouting-grade seeds (online or via specialty stores). Leafy vegetables and salad greens, sunflower, broccoli, mustard and cabbage are great plants for growing as microgreens. Some seeds are easier to grow than others. Cress, chia, teff and quinoa, for example, germinate and grow quickly, so they are great to start with, while others may take a bit of practice. Whole chia seeds (like flaxseeds) are often grown best as microgreens because they are mucilaginous, or have gel-like properties, that make soaking them for sprouting tricky because it often results in a gel instead of sprouts.

We suggest starting with a smaller amount of seeds until you become familiar with how they grow, as this will help avoid any waste. When you feel you have enough know-how, plant a large tray or multiple containers of microgreens.

Getting Your Microgreens Started

To begin, you will need either plastic food trays or containers with lids, or you can purchase sprouting trays from your local growing centre. With a little patience and practice, it is possible to plant microgreens in almost any container. You will also need your seeds, a spray bottle, potting soil, cheesecloth (optional), scissors or a knife and a piece of cardboard or newspaper to cover.

Microgreens can be grown inside or outdoors, but to ensure the best possible product, and avoid windblown dirt, feeding insects or local wildlife, we suggest indoors. To give the seeds the best possible start, soak them before planting. Although this is not necessary, it will save growing time. Soak quinoa, teff and chia for 12 hours before planting. Soak kañiwa and amaranth for 24 hours before planting. The following cheesecloth method will help you soak not only the regular seeds but also mucilaginous seeds, such as chia.

Cheesecloth Method

Cut a piece of cheesecloth that will fit inside the growing vessel, but make sure to double it up twice. You'll need to place seeds in the middle, like a sandwich with two layers of cheesecloth on each side of the seeds. Place the cloth on a rimmed baking sheet and open the cheesecloth into two halves. Sprinkle seeds sparingly (about ¼ inch/5 mm apart) and cover with the other half of the cloth. Gently pour water over the cheesecloth and seeds and let soak for the appropriate time (refer to specific package guidelines or the chart on page 12). The seeds and cheesecloth will need to be rinsed every 8 to 10 hours during that specified period. To do so, gently fold the cheesecloth into a manageable size and place in a fine mesh strainer. Rinse gently (to maintain water freshness and avoid rotting or premature deterioration) and allow to drain briefly. Gently unfold it back on the baking sheet and soak in water again. When the seeds have finished soaking, drain and place into your prepared growing vessel, on top of the soil (ensure there are holes in the bottom of the vessel for drainage and at least 1 inch/2.5 cm of moist organic potting soil in the bottom). Cover with a lid, cardboard or newspaper, leaving a

small opening for air circulation. Keep out of direct sunlight to prevent premature drying of soil. Water by spraying with the water bottle until moist but not soaked (you may not have to do this the first time you lay your cheese-cloth on the soil). The soil should always be moist to the touch but not soaking. Check the soil twice a day and spray with a water bottle, if necessary.

After the plants have grown to 1 inch (2.5 cm), remove the cover and place the vessel in partial or full sun. You may also choose to keep the vessel covered. It isn't necessary at this stage, but it helps keep the soil moist for longer. The seedlings will be ready to harvest when they are about 2 to 3 inches (5 to 7.5 cm) high. If your seedlings get too large, their texture and flavour may become less palatable. Harvest microgreens by cutting with scissors or a knife just above the cheesecloth.

Once the entire vessel of microgreens has been harvested, you will have to start over by removing the old stems, reworking the soil and planting again in a fresh piece of cheesecloth.

There are a few things to keep in mind while you are waiting for your microgreens to grow. Seeds will not grow if they are overwatered or under-watered, have poor air circulation, are planted too close together, are infertile or are pre-soaked too little or too long. Overwatering and poor circulation may cause mould, which will look like small spider webs, to appear on your microgreens. Some seeds will take longer to get started, so be patient. If your seeds don't grow at all, start over with different seeds. Some trial and error is involved, and a variety of methods can be found online. We encourage you to experiment with sprouting and growing your own microgreens!

PROTEIN OVERVIEW

When choosing to eliminate meat from recipes, or from your diet altogether, a major consideration is how to then consume enough protein. Protein is a requirement for many physiological processes, including building and maintaining tissues, such as muscle, cartilage and skin, and it's even necessary for the health of our bones, hormones and blood. Recommended protein intake for adults is anywhere from 10 to 35 percent of daily calories. Research debates continue on whether that is too much or not enough, but to keep your body healthy, the recommended amounts are a great start. Multiply your weight in pounds by 0.36 to give you a base number of grams. The higher your level of activity and the more your body needs to rebuild, the more protein you'll need. For example, a 125-pound (56 kilogram), inactive woman needs 45 grams of protein daily.

Proteins are either complete or incomplete, meaning they either have all eight essential amino acids or they do not. Complete proteins that contain all eight amino acids are the optimal choice in that you don't need to eat other proteins for your body to use the nutrition. (Some people refer to nine essential amino acids, which includes the semi-essential amino acid histidine that adults produce but is essential only for infants because their bodies are unable to produce it.) Eating an incomplete protein requires that you add the missing amino acids to make it complete. Eating a combination of amino acids from both incomplete and complete protein sources is ideal and often complementary.

Comparing Different Protein Sources

Although meat has traditionally been viewed as a primary protein source, many plant-based sources equally measure up. When preparing a vegetarian meal, it's important to remember that substitutes for meat are not necessarily exclusively chosen for their protein count. Ingredients are often selected for their flavour, texture and bite as they compare to meat. However, when eliminating meat from a dish, or from your diet altogether, you need to be aware of protein-rich sources to meet your daily requirements. Often, when multiple protein sources are combined, even small amounts of protein stack up quickly.

Here are protein values for many meatless ingredients you can incorporate into vegetarian cooking. The protein count of some items may surprise you, such as a stellar 15 grams per cup (250 mL) for black beans and the always impressive 22 grams per cup (250 mL) for edamame.

SOURCE OF PROTEIN	GRAMS PER SERVING (1 CUP/ 250 ML)
almonds, raw whole	30
avocado, chopped	3
beets, cooked	2.5
black beans, cooked	15
black bean noodles, cooked	25
black-eyed peas, cooked	10
bok choy, shredded	1
broccoli	4
Brussels sprouts	3
bulgur, cooked	5.5
butternut squash, cubes	1.5
carrots, sliced	1
cashews	18
cauliflower	2
cheese, Cheddar, crumbled	28
cheese, goat (chèvre), crumbled	33
chard	1
chia seeds (1 Tbsp/15 mL)	2
chia seeds (1 cup/250 mL)	28
chickpeas, cooked	12
cottage cheese, 2% creamed	25
dulse	6
edamame (soybeans)	22
egg (1 large)	7.5
eggplant, raw cubed	1
Ezekiel bread (per slice)	4
farro, cooked	14
freekeh, cooked	14
green peas, cooked	9

SOURCE OF PROTEIN	GRAMS PER SERVING (1 CUP/ 250 ML)
hemp seeds (1 Tbsp/15 mL)	4
hemp seeds (1 cup/250 mL)	53
lentils, cooked	18
low-fat milk, 1%	8
millet, cooked	7
nattō	30
parsnips, sliced	2
peanut butter (1 Tbsp/15 mL)	4
pecans, chopped	10
pistachios	26
polenta (cornmeal), cooked	4
portobello mushroom, chopped	2
pumpkin, cubed	1.5
quinoa, cooked	8
Quorn (mycoprotein)	26
seitan	63
soba noodles (100% buckwheat)	6
soy milk	8
spinach	4
spirulina (1 Tbsp/15 mL)	4
steel-cut oats	7
sweet potato	2
tempeh	30
tofu (soy protein)	20
walnuts	15
whole wheat bread (per slice)	3.5
wild rice	7
plain yogurt, 1%	10
zucchini, slices	1.5

BUDGET AND ACCESSIBILITY

It may not always be easy to find the meat substitutes you are looking for. Remote locations can limit vegetable selection and variety, and this often means these items can be quite pricey. But don't let your budget or location prevent you from eating meatless! Eat the options that are available to you and that you can afford.

There are simple substitutions for most ingre-dients—we've even replaced pumpkin with carrots before! If fresh is not available, consider other options, such as frozen or dehydrated veg-etables; dried mushrooms, grains, seeds, lentils and beans; frozen soy products; dried or frozen herbs; and even cheese. You may even opt for dehydrated sauce mixes, if necessary. Of course, these may not taste exactly the same as fresh, but they are budget-friendly and still flavourful. And you can always grow your own sprouts or microgreens!

HOW TO USE THIS BOOK

Some of the recipes in this book are tagged with one or more of four icons:

- GF Gluten-free
- DF Dairy-free
- V Vegan
- R Raw

Some recipes naturally fall into these catego-ries, and others have suggestions at the end of the recipes for preparing them to meet these requirements. These modifications may have necessary substitutions, additional options and instructions.

STOCKING YOUR VEGETARIAN PANTRY

Vegetarian meal preparation includes a range of delicious options. The list of available items in the grocery store continues to grow, and the possibilities are truly endless. Even if the selection in your area is restricted, we are sure you will find enough to prepare meatless meals that are full of flavour, in a variety of cooking styles from more traditional North American to Italian, Asian, fresh Californian, Eastern European, Mexican (one of our favourites) or a fusion of a number of these cuisines.

Meatless cooking incorporates a wide array of fresh fruits and vegetables, legumes, beans, sea vegetables, dairy, eggs, cheese, grains, seeds, nuts, herbs and spices. We'll show you how to use your favourite ingredients in new ways and entice you to add more unusual items to your kitchen pantry.

Plenty of nutritious alternatives have just as much substance as meat. We love incorporating savoury mushrooms into our favourite vegetarian meals. Large meaty ones like portobello or a woodsy, flavourful variety like shiitake or porcini are some of our favourite meat substitutes. Earthy root vegetables, such as sweet potatoes and beets, add superb flavour and colour, and provide a wonderfully hearty foundation for soups and many types of baked and roasted vegetarian dishes. Veggies like parsnip and turnip can also kick up the flavour profile

and are wonderful combined with other staple vegetables that might have a less assertive taste. And of course, legumes, beans, grains and noodles can offer ways to transform traditional dishes into delicious and impressive creations with new visual appeal and satisfying texture.

Cooking vegetarian meals allows you to play around and incorporate lots of vegetables and fruits into your dishes; however, it's important to note that toxic chemical sprays and treatments used in growing many plants today have raised concerns about the dangers of consuming these foods. We recommend avoiding chemically treated, genetically modified (GM) or genetically engineered (GE) foods by choosing products specifically labelled as certified organic and not genetically modified (non-GMO).

There are so many options for stocking your meatless pantry. We've highlighted many of our own favourites as a guide. Some may be more familiar to you than others, but there are plenty of suggestions for things you'll want to try.

Beans and Legumes

Beans and legumes are low-fat, nutrient-rich sources of protein and fibre. They are inexpensive and adaptable to many flavour profiles, making them versatile in all kinds of recipes. The variety of available beans and legumes is vast, and what you can't find in your local area

you could easily have shipped as dry beans, which don't require special treatment or storage and have a fairly long shelf-life. They can be soaked and sprouted, cooked and eaten whole, puréed or even found in flour form, and used in casseroles, dips, batters and soups.

- black beans
- chickpeas (garbanzo beans)
- edamame (soybeans)
- green peas
- kidney beans red and white
- lentils beluga, green and red
- lima beans
- navy beans
- pinto beans

Dairy and Eggs

An essential kitchen staple for many, butter is more than a tasty and practical choice; the human body knows how to digest and use it, unlike other chemical and processed fats. Even a small amount of butter or cheese can add a blast of flavour and texture to complete a dish. Nutrient-rich eggs and milk offer protein and calcium, and add moisture and thickening when needed. They're a tremendously nutritious, non-meat protein source, that contain all of the amino acids your body needs, which makes them an essential pantry item for meatless cooking. Yogurt, on its own or added into dishes, is a tasty way of helping provide beneficial gut flora to the digestive system.

- butter
- cheese Cheddar, Colby, cottage, Farmers, feta, goat, halloumi, Havarti, Parmesan and Romano
- clarified butter (ghee)
- eggs
- milk buttermilk, cow, goat and sheep (for non-dairy milks, see Milk Alternatives, page 21)
- plain yogurt (no gelatin, with live cultures)
- sour cream

Fermented Foods

Fermented is back! Often overlooked until recently, fermented foods have health benefits and dominant flavours that can dramatically elevate the personality of meatless recipes. Available in a variety of unique sources, fermented ingredients contain beneficial gut bacteria that support optimal digestion and disease resistance.

- black garlic
- kefir
- kimchi
- miso
- sauerkraut
- sourdough
- tempeh

Fruits and Vegetables

Fresh, steamed, grilled or roasted, the plethora of nature's produce available today makes meatless cooking diverse, nutritious and inspiring. Vegetables and fruit can serve as the foundation for dishes, while some are used to season, garnish or complement other flavours and textures. The advantage of grilling vegetables rather than meat is that any harmful chemicals that may be created from cooking or charring meat do not occur in vegetables.

- apples
- avocados
- bell peppers
- berries açai, blackberries, blueberries, cranberries, goji, strawberries and raspberries
- bok choy baby, regular and
- Shanghai
- broccoli, rapini
- Brussels sprouts
- cabbage Chinese, green, red and savoy
- cauliflower
- celeriac
- celery
- chard green and red

- **citrus fruits**
  grapefruits, lemons, limes, mandarins, oranges and tangerines
- **collard greens**
- **cucumbers**
- **daikon**
- **dandelion greens**
- **dates**
- **eggplants**
- **fennel**
- **figs**
- **garlic**
- **kale**
  black and green
- **kiwis**
- **leeks**
- **lettuce**
  arugula, butter, endive, iceberg, radicchio, red and romaine
- **mangoes**

- **melons**
  cantaloupe, honeydew and watermelon
- **onions**
  green, red, shallots and yellow
- **papayas**
- **plums**
- **pomegranates**
- **root vegetables**
  beets, carrots, parsnips, potatoes, radishes, rutabagas, sweet potatoes and turnips
- **spinach**
- **sprouts**
- **squash**
  acorn, butternut, pumpkin, spaghetti and zucchini
- **tomatoes**
  canned or fresh

Mushrooms

Mushrooms are pleasantly chewy with enough substance and gusto to easily stand in for meat. Grilled, sliced, ground, puréed or whole, they aren't shy on flavour. With great nutritional value that is often understated, mushrooms are also a low-calorie, no-fat choice that makes them a most qualified alternative.

- **button**
- **chanterelles**
- **cremini**
- **enoki**
- **morels**

- **oyster**
- **porcini**
- **portobello**
- **shiitake**
- **trumpet**

Grains and Seeds

Non-genetically modified grains and seeds, especially ancient varieties, can be nutritious sources of lean, non-animal protein, including many that are even complete proteins all on their own. Many forms are available—from groats and whole grains to flours, flakes and puffs—to extend their application even further. Full of antioxidants and fibre, each has its own esteemed list of health benefits. Grains and seeds can play the main role in a recipe or serve as a reliable side, and they are suited to many meal personalities—they can be dressed up with a whole realm of flavours and used in many international cuisines.

- **amaranth**
- **barley**
- **black rice**
- **brown rice**
- **buckwheat**
- **bulgur**
- **chia**
- **farro**
- **freekeh**
- **hemp**
- **Kamut**
- **kañiwa**
- **millet**
- **nattō**

- **oats**
  quick, rolled or old-fashioned and steel-cut
- **quinoa**
- **Quorn**
  (mycoprotein)
- **red rice**
- **sesame (tahini)**
- **sorghum**
- **spelt**
- **sunflower**
  butter and seeds
- **teff**
- **wheat berries**
- **white rice**
- **wild rice**

Milk Alternatives

Finding dairy-free milk is easy nowadays, with a wide range of these alternatives readily available in supermarkets and health food stores. This trusty cooking assistant can be used to blend ingredients in casseroles, soups, sauces

and dressings. Without overpowering recipes, these milks can inject another touch of nutrition, create smoothness and even deepen or intensify flavours. Many of them can be made easily in your own kitchen so you can make them free of additives and preservatives.

- almond
- cashew
- coconut
- flax
- hazelnut
- hemp
- oat
- macadamia nut
- rice
- soy

Nuts and Nut Butters

Nuts have become an invaluable staple in vegetarian cooking. Not only are they full of healthy fats, vitamins and minerals, but they're delicious raw or toasted, as an added ingredient or a snack all on their own. They can be used to make nut butters or soaked and puréed to make milks, sauces, dressings and even cheese! Cooking them minimally, if at all, helps to preserve their superb nutrition.

- almond
- cashew
- hazelnut
- peanut
- pine nut
- pistachio
- walnut

Oils and Vinegars

Together, oils and vinegars are often combined to create dressings and dips. Alone, oil is regularly used to augment cooking and can provide doses of healthy fats for the body. Many vinegars also have health benefits and can do a great job of adding a necessary pungent note to a dish where required.

- apple cider vinegar
- coconut oil
- extra virgin olive oil
- grapeseed oil
- balsamic vinegar
  red and white
- rice vinegar
- sesame oil
- wine vinegar
  red and white

Pasta and Noodles

Pasta and noodles used as a meal staple is really nothing new. They make such a great meal because they hold their own as a substantial part of the plate and can be made to suit almost any taste. With the increasing selection of noodles and pasta available in the market today, conventional pasta is getting a makeover! All the usual shapes and cuts are being fortified and some remade completely with more healthful ingredients, including ancient and whole grains, beans and legumes, vegetables, sea vegetables, even Chinese medicinals and almost every source of antioxidant. Major grocery stores have large selections and any Asian grocery will have an exciting range of noodles and other pastas that contain everything from green tea to blue algae, mushrooms, miso, bamboo, charcoal, pumpkin and more. This widely used meal ingredient now has even more possibilities!

- black bean noodles
- quinoa noodles
- rice vermicelli
  brown rice and spinach rice
- soba noodles (buckwheat)
- sourdough noodles
- whole-grain (wheat) noodles

Sea Vegetables

Sea vegetables can add a new flavour experience to recipes and, as such, work well and have a long history in many vegetarian dishes and international cuisines. Even small amounts are loaded with nutrients, and they can provide powerful cancer and antiviral phytonutrients and trace minerals, as well as the most concentrated food source of iodine. Not just used to wrap sushi, the brackish taste of sea vegetables can be extremely appealing in soups, stews, salads and noodle dishes, and alongside spicy, sweet or tangy flavours. The salty taste sea vegetables provide means you can reduce additional salt elsewhere in your recipes.

- agar-agar
- arame
- dulse
- hijiki
- kombu
- kudzu
- laver
- nori
- spirulina

Spices and Seasonings

Spices and seasonings provide the perfect tools for infusing flavour and identity into recipes. An abundance of vastly different options gives any cook an extensive line-up with which to create. Often they originate from a single source; others are made from combinations of herbs and spices. Spices and seasonings may complement or compete with each other, so they're chosen wisely and generally used sparingly.

- **bouillon**
  vegetable
- **cardamom**
- **cloves**
- **coriander**
- **cumin**
- **dashi**
  kombu or shiitake
- **fresh herbs**
  basil, bay leaf, chives, cilantro, dill, mint, oregano, parsley, rosemary, sage, savoury and thyme
- **ginger**
- **ground pepper**
  ancho, black, chili, chipotle and white
- **herbs de Provence**
- **honey**
- **hot sauce**
  Sriracha
- **juniper berries**
- **lemongrass**
- **maple syrup**
- **marjoram**
- **mustard**
- **nutmeg**
- **nutritional yeast**
- **paprika and smoked paprika**
- **salt**
  black, kosher, pink and sea
- **shichimi togarashi**
- **soy sauce**
- **sumac**
- **tamari**
- **turmeric**
- **vanilla**
- **wasabi powder**
- **Worcestershire sauce (vegan)**
- **za'atar**

Tofu and Meat Substitutes

These protein-rich meat substitutes made from plant sources often mimic many of the same characteristics of conventional meat products in texture, bite and varying levels of moisture.

- **seitan**
- **tofu**

THE ESSENTIAL TOOLS

A number of essential cooking tools help make vegetarian cooking efficient, simple and look and taste great. You don't have to buy them all—their importance will vary depending on your interest and skill level. Undoubtedly, you already have many of these tools in your kitchen.

Baking sheets and roasting pans Roasting, grilling and baking vegetables often requires larger, flat pans for space to spread out and promote even cooking. They're relatively inexpensive, so having a few on hand ensures you won't have to shuffle ingredients around too much, especially in those veggie-loaded recipes.

Barbecue Outdoor barbecue grills are great for achieving a "meaty," smoky flavour that comes from grilling and charring over fire. Barbecues help develop the flavour profile, so they mimic, equal or trump the satisfaction and substance of cooking meat on the grill.

Cheesecloth This gauze-like cloth is used for draining and fine-straining vegetables, and it's an essential tool in making your own condiments, yogurt and stocks and in growing microgreens.

Cheese slicer A handheld cheese slicer is a decorative slicing tool when placed on a marble slab or wooden board and used for thinly slicing firm and semi-firm cheeses. We find these useful in slicing perfect paper-thin ribbons of vegetables, which are great for layered salads, for fancy sandwiches or as faux pasta.

Cooking string This essential tool can be used for tying whole herbs in a bundle, called a bouquet garni, to immerse in broths, soups and stocks.

Cutting boards You will find having multiple cutting boards on hand in a busy kitchen is necessary to chop vegetables, nuts, fruits and herbs. Wooden or bamboo boards are heavy and solid and made of natural materials but require some care, such as handwashing. Moulded plastic boards are less porous and won't retain the strong flavours, scents or bacteria certain ingredients may leave behind. They can usually be washed and sanitized in the dishwasher.

Dutch oven This large, usually cast-iron or other heavy metal, cooking pot has a tight-fitting lid to seal in flavour and keep an even temperature while cooking. These are great for the stovetop or oven and especially for casseroles and one-pot meals. They are the perfect vessel for braising, sautéing, searing, stewing and simmering.

High-speed or professional blender A quality, high-speed professional blender may be expensive, but it is an appliance you will have for a lifetime. It will not only save time and effort but can also enhance your meatless dishes in ways you never thought possible. A high-quality blender can help in achieving super-smooth purées for soups, sauces, dips, and blending up fresh cooked vegetables, beans, legumes, fruits and more. Once you start using it, you'll wonder how you ever lived without it. Vitamix and Blendtec are popular brands.

Immersion blender An immersion blender is a great time-saving tool that eliminates a lot of fuss in the kitchen. If you're cooking a hot soup or sauce, for example, you can simply plug in the immersion blender and purée your ingredients in the pot, on the stovetop. This reduces the hassle and danger of an injury in moving hot soup to a blender or food processor, and it saves time since you don't have to cool or reheat ingredients.

Julienne slicer A julienne slicer looks like a vegetable peeler, but has additional blades to create straight matchstick or julienne slices of carrots, beets, apples, cucumbers, zucchini and even hard cheese like Parmesan cheese.

Knives Even one or two quality knives will do most of the jobs in your kitchen. A good chef's knife has multiple uses and will become your new best friend for chopping vegetables and slicing fruit, cheese and almost anything else! Paring knives are useful for peeling, trimming or slicing smaller items.

Mandoline slicer A mandoline is great for slicing medium to hard fruit, such as apples and pears, as well as vegetables like carrots, beets, cucumbers, tomatoes and potatoes. Most mandolines allow you to choose the thickness of the slice if you need to change it up for salads, sandwiches, casseroles or desserts. A mandoline can also cut a beautiful julienne slice or thin ribbons without a fuss. These tools can be dangerous—just ask Carolyn—so we caution you to always use a guard or another tool when slicing hard or awkwardly shaped foods over that razor-sharp blade! Clean up is easy: all it takes is a careful, quick rinse or brush when done. Mandolines are especially useful if you have a large amount of slicing to do.

Skillets Skillets or large, wide-bottomed saucepans, especially seasoned cast-iron skillets, are great for achieving that savoury flavour that's created when browning, caramelizing, reducing, searing and sautéing. Especially with onions and mushrooms, cooking in a skillet can help develop the rich flavour profile you would expect in a favourite meaty meal.

Small food processor You may have a large version, but having a mini or small food processor can be useful for quickly grinding nuts, grains and vegetables. It's also a key tool when preparing dips, butters, sauces, seasonings and soups. When you're pressed for time, these processors can quickly chop ingredients like fresh herbs, onions or garlic.

Spiralizers This kitchen tool can be found in handheld and freestanding models and creates thin, spaghetti-like, spiralized cuts of fruits, such as apples, and vegetables, such as beets, carrots, potatoes, zucchini and cucumbers. Handheld versions are best for smaller jobs and generally don't have interchangeable blades. Freestanding units can cope with larger quantities, like when slicing zucchini pasta, and generally come with an array of blades to slice in varying thicknesses. Spiralizers, especially standalone types, can mean a bit more clean-up compared with smaller handheld devices, but it is worth it for perfect, consistent cuts and bigger batch recipes.

Standard vegetable or fruit peeler Almost everyone has a standard "potato" peeler in the kitchen. You can do much more with these tools than just peel, however! Sharpened peelers can create simple curls and ribbons of vegetables, such as beets, carrots, potatoes, root vegetables and cucumber. Apples and other fruits can be peeled into thin strips as well. Flakes, petals or curls of hard cheeses such as Parmesan make a great salad topper.

Strainers Having a number of different-sized strainers can be useful. Large strainers are useful when rinsing or cleaning big batches or bulkier raw vegetables, rinsing tofu and draining beans or cooked vegetables. Smaller, fine mesh strainers are necessary when rinsing herbs, grains and seeds or straining liquids.

Wave slicer or knife This small knife or chopper is terrific for creating waves in foods like cucumbers, carrots and cheeses. Wavy choppers can also be used by children (under proper supervision) to bring some fun to cutting up cheese, apple slices and a whole host of raw vegetables.

Whisks A favourite of ours, whisks are the ultimate, easy-to-grab hand blenders. They can be made of bamboo, plastic or metal, but we always opt for the strong metal variety. Great for quickly mixing soups or sauces, they can also blend flours and other dry ingredients quickly and thoroughly.

Zesters and rasps Zesters are handy for removing the perfect thickness of citrus rind from the skin without pulling off the bitter pith. Rasps can also be used for zesting citrus and finely grating hard cheeses like Parmesan.

SMALL PLATES
AND
SIDE DISHES

FIRE ROASTED SALSA WITH HOME BAKED TORTILLA CHIPS

Sweet red pepper, roasted over a barbecue, takes salsa to a whole different level. Any salsa or chip lover will enjoy this flavour combination. Make your own tortilla chips to avoid excessive salt and oil in the store-bought versions. If you can't find corn tortillas, try rice tortillas or use whole wheat if you don't require them to be gluten-free. You can easily double or triple this recipe for group events.

Serves 4 **DF** **GF** **V**

HOME BAKED TORTILLA CHIPS
6 small (6-inch/15 cm) corn tortillas
1 Tbsp (15 mL) grapeseed oil
Pinch of sea salt

FIRE ROASTED SALSA
1 sweet red pepper, halved
   lengthwise, seeds and
   stem removed
3 large (1 lb/450 g)
   Roma tomatoes, diced
1½ Tbsp (22 mL) minced
   Spanish onion
4 tsp (20 mL) chopped fresh cilantro
1 tsp (5 mL) olive oil
½ tsp (2 mL) minced garlic
Squeeze of fresh lime juice
Pinch of sea salt

Preheat the oven to 325°F (160°C). Line one large or two small baking sheets with parchment paper and set aside.

Lightly brush each side of the tortillas with grapeseed oil. Stack the six tortillas on a cutting board and cut into eight wedges with a pizza cutter or sharp knife. Spread the wedges in a single layer on baking sheets. Sprinkle with salt. Bake in the oven for about 7 to 8 minutes. Remove from the oven and stir. Bake for another 7 to 8 minutes or until lightly golden and dry. Remove from the oven and set aside to cool.

Preheat a barbecue to about 600°F (300°C). Place the red pepper skin side down on the grill. Barbecue until the skin has blackened about 75 percent, which will take 10 to 15 minutes. Remove the pepper from the grill, but retain the blackened outer skin.

Dice the pepper flesh with the blackened skin and toss in a bowl with the tomatoes, onion, cilantro, olive oil, garlic, lime juice and salt. Let the salsa sit for 30 minutes to develop the flavour. Serve with the chips and enjoy.

> TIP: Don't have a barbecue? Roast red peppers skin side up on a foil-lined baking sheet in the oven under the broiler until the skin has blackened.

ROASTED VEGETABLE DIP WITH CRUDITÉS

Roasted vegetables seasoned and puréed make a uniquely different spread from the usual options for sandwiches or veggies, crackers and cheese. This is a great option if you're having a party or feeding a crowd—the recipe can be doubled easily and made up to 2 days in advance.

Makes 1 cup (250 mL)

1 sweet red pepper, halved lengthwise, seeds and stem removed

½ lb (225 g) eggplant, cut into slices ½ inch (1 cm) thick (peel the eggplant if it's large)

1 Tbsp (15 mL) grapeseed oil

Pinch of sea salt

Pinch of pepper

1 large shallot, chopped

2 tsp (10 mL) white or regular balsamic vinegar

¼ tsp (1 mL) chopped garlic

Preheat the oven to 425°F (220°C). Line a large baking sheet with parchment paper.

Place the red pepper halves and eggplant slices on the prepared baking sheet. Brush the vegetables with the oil and sprinkle with a pinch of salt and pepper. Cook for 20 minutes or until vegetables are roasted and tender. Set aside to cool completely.

Place the vegetables (including the charred pepper skins), shallots, vinegar and garlic in a blender or food processor until almost smooth or very smooth, whichever you prefer. Season with additional salt and pepper if desired. Refrigerate for up to 5 days.

TIP: 1. If you don't require the dip to be dairy-free or vegan, for a creamier version, process 4 oz (115 g) of cream cheese in with the vegetables. If you want it creamier and vegan or dairy-free, soak ½ cup (125 mL) of cashews in water for 30 minutes, then rinse. Purée soaked cashews in a high-speed blender and process puréed cashews in with the vegetables. 2. Instead of eggplant, you can use an equal amount of zucchini. Roast the vegetables 10 minutes longer to ensure there is not too much moisture in the dip.

VEGETABLE NORI WRAPS
WITH ORANGE GINGER MISO DRESSING

Looking for a delicious appetizer that also happens to be healthy? Look no further. Vegetable nori wraps not only look fresh but are a great appetizer or addition to any kind of meal. Cut the vegetables into matchsticks with a knife, or use a spiralizer for a dramatic effect. Make the dressing and cut the vegetables in advance, then simply assemble just before serving. The Asian flavours here pair really nicely with the Hot Bok Choy and Shiitake Mushroom Soup with Black Garlic (page 67).

Makes 16 wraps

ORANGE GINGER MISO DRESSING

¾ cup (175 mL) unsweetened orange juice
3 Tbsp (45 mL) chopped yellow onion
3 Tbsp (45 mL) vegetable oil
1 Tbsp (15 mL) white or yellow miso
1½ tsp (7 mL) apple cider vinegar
1¼ tsp (6 mL) finely grated fresh ginger
Black sesame seeds, to garnish

VEGETABLE NORI WRAPS

4 sheets of sushi nori (dried seaweed sheets), each cut into 4 equal squares
4 large carrots, peeled and cut into 5-inch (12.5 cm) long matchsticks
¾ cup (175 mL) sprouts or shoots of your choice
1 large red beet, peeled and cut into 5-inch (12.5 cm) long matchsticks

Place orange juice, onion, oil, miso, vinegar and ginger in a blender, and process until smooth. Pour into a serving dish, cover and top with a sprinkle of black sesame seeds. Refrigerate until serving.

Evenly space the wraps flat on a clean work surface. Place about 6 carrot matchsticks diagonally on each piece of the nori. Then place about 2 tablespoons (30 mL) of sprouts or shoots on top of the carrots, and top with about 6 beet matchsticks. Dip the tip of your finger in water and use the moisture to glue the two opposite corners of the nori together. Place on a serving tray or individual plates. Repeat with remaining ingredients. Serve with the dressing for dipping.

GLUTEN-FREE OPTION Replace the miso with gluten-free miso.

RAW OPTION Choose unpasteurized miso and raw untoasted nori.

FRESH STUFFED AVOCADOS

Filled with a mixture of cottage cheese, diced cucumber, fresh dill and a squeeze of lime juice, these avocados have a simple, meal-ready attitude that only requires a fork. Al fresco, picnic or barbecue worthy—this light and lively dish will remind you of summer weather, even in winter. These avocados would pair nicely with the Ancho Tempeh Chili (page 82).

Serves 4 **GF**

2 whole avocados
1 cup (250 mL) 1% cottage cheese
¼ cup (60 mL) finely diced
   cucumber
2 Tbsp (30 mL) chopped
   fresh dill
1 tsp (5 mL) fresh lime juice
Pinch of black Himalayan sea salt or
   other sea salt (optional)

Slice the avocados lengthwise, remove the stone and set them aside.

In a medium bowl, mix the cottage cheese, cucumber, dill and lime juice. Place ¼ cup (60 mL) scoop of the cottage cheese mixture inside the middle of each avocado half. Serve with a small sprinkle of salt on top (if using).

> TIP: A great way to tell if your avocado is perfectly ripe is by lifting off the small stem cap at the top of the avocado. If you lift it away and it is green underneath, you have a freshly ripe avocado. If it is brown underneath, it is over-ripe. If it won't easily lift off, it is not yet ready to eat.

MUSHROOM AND FARRO ROMAINE HEARTS

Toasted farro along with shiitake and portobello mushrooms are mixed with sautéed shallots, garlic and ginger, spiked with miso, and then we kick it up a notch with a shot of hot sauce and a sprinkle of toasted cashews. Served on a crunchy romaine heart leaf, this dish is a wonderful mix of freshness and savoury flavour. For a perfect meal, serve alongside Hot Bok Choy and Shiitake Mushroom Soup with Black Garlic (page 67).

Serves 4 **DF** **V**

⅓ cup (75 mL) chopped cashews
1 Tbsp (15 mL) grapeseed oil
⅓ cup (75 mL) chopped shallots
1½ cups (375 mL) chopped shiitake
   mushrooms, stems removed
1½ cups (375 mL) chopped
   portobello mushrooms,
   stems removed
1 tsp (5 mL) minced garlic
½ cup (125 mL) farro
1½ cups (375 mL) water
1 Tbsp (15 mL) minced fresh ginger
½ Tbsp (7 mL) yellow or red miso
1 Tbsp (15 mL) red cooking wine
2 tsp (10 mL) Sriracha hot sauce
¼ tsp (1 mL) sea salt
2 heads romaine hearts, leaves
   separated, washed and dried

Heat a large saucepan on medium heat and place the cashews in the pan. Stir frequently until the cashews are fragrant and toasted. Remove from the heat, cool slightly and set aside.

Place the oil and shallots in the saucepan and cook until soft and translucent. Add the mushrooms and garlic, and continue to cook until soft. If saucepan is dry, add a few drops more of oil or some water.

Add the farro and stir gently to lightly toast and combine. Add the water and bring to a boil, then reduce the heat to a simmer and continue to cook, covered, for 25 to 30 minutes or until farro is tender and no liquid remains in the saucepan.

Whisk together the ginger, miso, wine, hot sauce and salt in a small bowl. Add to the farro-mushroom mixture in the saucepan and stir well. Serve 1 to 2 Tbsp (15 to 30 mL) scoops of the farro-mushroom mixture on top of each romaine leaf. Sprinkle with toasted cashews and serve.

GLUTEN-FREE OPTION Replace the miso with gluten-free miso.

> TIP: Don't have farro on hand? This recipe would also be great with quinoa, wheat berries or red or black heirloom rice.

CRISPY BUFFALO CAULIFLOWER BITES

Craving buffalo hot wings? We've made these buffalo cauliflower bites taste as authentic as possible using some clever tricks with millet flour and nutritional yeast. But keep that a secret and make two batches—because they'll go fast.

Serves 4 as a side or 8 as an appetizer GF

⅓ cup (75 mL) millet flour

⅓ cup (75 mL) nutritional yeast

½ cup (125 mL) water

1 head of cauliflower, cut into
   bite-sized pieces

¼ cup (60 mL) Louisiana hot sauce

½ cup (125 mL) Blue Cheese Dip
   (page 198) or Herbed Kefir Ranch
   Dressing (see page 102)

2 stalks celery, cut into sticks

2 large carrots, cut into sticks

Preheat the oven to 425°F (220°C). Line one large or two small baking sheets with parchment paper and set aside.

Whisk together the flour, nutritional yeast and water until smooth. Toss with the cauliflower in a large bowl until evenly coated. Spread evenly in a single layer on the prepared baking sheet and bake for 15 minutes.

Remove from the oven and quickly toss with the hot sauce. Return to the oven for another 5 minutes or until the sauce has baked onto cauliflower. Serve the bites immediately with dressing and vegetable sticks.

BLUSHING BEET AND BLUE CHEESE DEVILED EGGS WITH TOASTED PECANS

Deviled eggs this pretty are eye-catching and a bit out of the ordinary with the full-flavour of blue cheese and roasted pecans. Traditional mayonnaise is replaced with Greek yogurt, meaning fewer calories with just as much flavour as conventional deviled eggs. But remember to start on these ahead of time—the eggs need 8 hours of immersion to become blushed and beautiful.

Makes 24 deviled eggs

12 large eggs
3 cups (750 mL) water
1 cup (250 mL) white pickling vinegar
1 cup (250 mL) peeled and chopped red beets
2 Tbsp (30 mL) liquid honey
2 shallots, chopped
¼ tsp (1 mL) sea salt
24 pecan halves
⅓ cup (75 mL) plain Greek yogurt
⅓ cup (75 mL) crumbled blue cheese
1 Tbsp (15 mL) chopped fresh thyme
3 Tbsp (45 mL) microgreens (optional)

GLUTEN-FREE OPTION Choose blue cheese and pickling vinegar that are gluten-free.

TIP: Use the additional cooked egg yolks in your favourite salads, sandwiches or noodle and fried rice dishes.

Place the whole eggs, in their shells, in a large saucepan with enough water to cover them. Bring to a boil and cover with lid. Turn the heat off and leave covered on the burner for 13 minutes. Remove from the heat and discard the hot water. Cover the eggs with ice cold water and set aside to cool. Remove the shells when the eggs are completely cool, and place them in either one 8-cup (2 L) or two 4-cup (1 L) canning jars.

Bring 3 cups (750 mL) of water, vinegar, beets, honey, shallots and salt to a simmer over medium-low heat. Cover and simmer for 20 minutes. Remove from the heat and allow to cool completely. Pour the mixture over the eggs in the canning jars. Seal the jars with their lids, and refrigerate for 8 hours or up to 2 days. (Left too long, the yolk also turns purple, which does not look appealing.)

Preheat the oven to 350°F (180°C) and evenly spread the pecan halves on a baking sheet. Toast the pecans in the oven for 5 to 7 minutes or until lightly toasted and fragrant. Set aside to cool.

Remove the pickled eggs from the jars and place on a paper towel for a minute to dry. Gently slice the eggs lengthwise and carefully remove the yolks. Place the egg white halves on a serving tray.

Place 6 full yolks into a medium bowl and mash with a fork. Mix in the yogurt and blue cheese. Scoop the filling into a plastic resealable bag and cut ¾-inch (2 cm) off one corner, or place the filling in a plastic piping bag (without a tip). Pipe about 1 tsp (5 mL) of filling into each of the egg halves. Stand a toasted pecan half in the middle of the filling and sprinkle each egg with fresh thyme and microgreens (if using). Serve immediately.

BLACK QUINOA AND CAULIFLOWER
HALLOUMI CHEESE BALLS

Crisp on the outside and chewy-soft on the inside, these savoury quinoa cauliflower balls deliver on taste. Cauliflower, black quinoa, halloumi cheese and garlic make these tasty morsels a great tapas selection, finger-food appetizer or side dish along with the Tossed Baby Arugula and Zucchini Salad (page 90).

Makes 35 1-inch (2.5 cm) balls, serves 6 to 8

1 cup (250 mL) Simple Vegetable Broth (page 62) or low-sodium, store-bought vegetable broth

½ cup (125 mL) black quinoa or red, rainbow or white/golden quinoa

1 large egg

1½ cups (375 mL) finely grated, firmly packed cauliflower

1 cup (250 mL) shredded halloumi cheese

¼ cup (60 mL) oat flour

1 tsp (5 mL) minced garlic

1 tsp (5 mL) nutritional yeast

1 tsp (5 mL) fresh lemon juice

¼ tsp (1 mL) ground black pepper

¼ tsp (1 mL) ground nutmeg

¼ tsp (1 mL) sea salt

Preheat the oven to 375°F (190°C). Line a large baking sheet with parchment paper and set aside.

Combine the broth and quinoa in a medium saucepan and bring to a boil. Reduce to a simmer, cover and cook for 15 minutes. Remove from the heat and let sit, covered, for another 15 minutes. Fluff with a fork and set aside to cool.

In a medium bowl, beat the egg and add the cooked quinoa, cauliflower, halloumi cheese, flour, garlic, nutritional yeast, lemon juice, pepper, nutmeg and salt. Scoop 1 Tbsp (15 mL) balls onto prepared baking sheet. Bake in the oven for 25 to 30 minutes or until the bottom edges are golden brown. Remove from the baking sheet and let cool slightly. Serve warm.

> TIP: Make oat flour quickly by grinding up quick or large-flake oats in your food processor or high-speed blender. Ensure you buy oats clearly labelled *gluten-free*, if you require it.

SPICY QUINOA FRIES WITH GINGER CARROT DIP

Crispy yet chewy, these mini breadstick "fries" are made with puréed and baked quinoa, cut into strips and spiced from the inside out. Dipped in a tangy Japanese-inspired ginger carrot sauce, these fries are a perfect side or party food. If you want to double this batch, we recommend you don't use a bigger baking pan, rather two 8-inch (2 L) square baking pans. These fries are a great addition to the Coconut Chili Lime Collard Green Wraps (page 123).

Serves 4

SPICY QUINOA FRIES
1 cup (250 mL) water
½ cup (125 mL) white or
    golden quinoa
1 large egg
2 Tbsp (30 mL) 1% milk
1 Tbsp (15 mL) shichimi togarashi
    seasoning (see Tip)

GINGER CARROT DIP
½ cup (125 mL) coarsely
    chopped carrot
2 Tbsp (30 mL) grapeseed oil
2 Tbsp (30 mL) apple cider vinegar
2 Tbsp (30 mL) pure maple syrup
1 Tbsp (15 mL) soy sauce
1 Tbsp (15 mL) chopped white or
    yellow onion
1 tsp (5 mL) grated fresh ginger
Pinch of ground black pepper

Preheat the oven to 450°F (230°C). Line one 8-inch (2 L) square baking pan with parchment paper and set aside.

Bring the water and quinoa to a boil in a small saucepan. Reduce to a simmer, cover and cook for 15 minutes. Remove from the heat. Keep covered for an additional 15 minutes (the quinoa should be fully cooked and fluffy). Place the quinoa in a blender or food processor with the egg, milk and seasoning. Purée until completely smooth.

Spread evenly in the prepared pan and bake for 25 to 30 minutes or until the edges are crispy and golden. Remove from the oven, and with a sharp knife, cut into 3- × ½-inch (8 × 1 cm) strips. Return to the same pan (or use a separate baking sheet if desired) and bake for 5 more minutes to crisp-fry the edges.

Place the carrot, oil, vinegar, syrup, soy sauce, onion, ginger and black pepper in a blender or food processor. Purée until smooth. Serve as a dipping sauce with piping hot quinoa fries.

DAIRY-FREE OPTION Replace the milk with almond, hemp, soy or rice milk.

GLUTEN-FREE OPTION Replace the soy sauce with gluten-free tamari.

> TIP: Make your own shichimi togarashi seasoning! In a small food processor or blender, grind 2 tsp (10 mL) each of white and black sesame seeds and chili flakes. Add 1 tsp (5 mL) each of black peppercorns, hemp seeds, roasted orange zest, salt, ½ sheet of nori and ½ tsp (2 mL) of ground ginger. Grind as fine as possible. This seasoning will keep fresh for up to 2 weeks.

BAKED EGGPLANT CHIPS
WITH LIME MISO YOGURT DIP

Japanese eggplant slices are transformed into delicious "chips" when coated in a thin bread-crumb coating and baked crisp and tender. These are perfect as a light snack, side or tapas dish served with a zesty (and addictive!) miso dipping sauce full of rich garlic and fresh lime flavour. These savoury little bites are terrific eaten with the Grilled Pineapple Teriyaki Burgers (page 140).

Serves 4

BAKED EGGPLANT CHIPS
1 large egg
½ cup (125 mL) panko breadcrumbs
½ cup (125 mL) grated
   Parmesan cheese
3 cups (750 mL) Japanese eggplant,
   sliced into ⅛-inch (3 mm) rounds

LIME MISO YOGURT DIP
1 cup (250 mL) Natural Plain Yogurt
   (page 195) or store-bought
2 tsp (10 mL) red, white or yellow
   miso
2 tsp (10 mL) fresh lime juice
1 tsp (5 mL) fresh lime zest
½ tsp (2 mL) minced garlic

Preheat the oven to 350°F (180°C). Line a large baking sheet with parchment paper and set aside.

Beat the egg in a small bowl and set aside. Combine the breadcrumbs and Parmesan cheese, and place in a flat dish beside the bowl with the egg. Dip each eggplant slice into the egg first, then into the bread-crumb mixture. Place in a single layer on the baking sheet, and continue with the remaining eggplant slices. Bake in the oven for 25 to 30 minutes or until crispy and golden.

Mix the yogurt, miso, lime juice, zest and garlic in a medium bowl and place in the refrigerator until the eggplant chips are baked. Serve chips hot along with the chilled dipping sauce. The sauce will stay fresh for 1 to 2 days stored in the refrigerator.

GLUTEN-FREE OPTION Replace the panko breadcrumbs with fine, gluten-free breadcrumbs and the miso with gluten-free miso.

> TIP: Using a flat plate for breading the eggplant slices ensures the breadcrumbs stay even and do not become lumpy and unusable.

MAPLE MISO GLAZED BRUSSELS SPROUTS
AND CARROTS WITH TOASTED PECANS

Tender Brussels sprouts and carrots are lightly glazed with maple, miso, orange juice and a touch of butter and sprinkled with toasted pecans. This makes for a wonderful dish to accompany any meal or serve buffet-style at brunches or parties. Easily prepare in advance of dinner and simply reheat by covering in foil, and heating in the oven for 15 minutes at 325°F (160°C), then sprinkle with nuts just before serving. This dish is the ideal partner for the Pepper-Crusted Mushroom Steaks (page 160) or the Parsnip, Cauliflower and Potato Mash (page 49).

Serves 6 to 10

½ cup (125 mL) chopped pecans
2 Tbsp (30 mL) grapeseed oil
1½ lbs (680 g) Brussels sprouts,
   trimmed and halved through core
1 lb (450 g) carrots, peeled and
   cut into ¼-inch (5 mm) slices
   on an angle
⅔ cup (150 mL) peeled and
   chopped shallots
¾ cup (175 mL) water
1 tsp (5 mL) minced garlic
½ tsp (2 mL) sea salt
½ cup (125 mL) fresh orange juice
1 Tbsp (15 mL) pure maple syrup
2 tsp (10 mL) white or yellow (shiro)
   miso
1 tsp (5 mL) cornstarch
1 Tbsp (15 mL) unsalted butter

Heat a dry, large, heavy-bottomed saucepan or Dutch oven over medium-high heat. Place the pecans in the pan, stirring occasionally for about 4 to 6 minutes or until toasted and fragrant. Remove from the pan and place in a bowl to cool. Set aside.

Return the same pan to medium-high heat. Add the oil and Brussels sprouts. Tossing frequently, cook until some of the edges are golden (about 5 minutes). Add the carrots, shallots, water, garlic and salt. Cover and cook for 8 to 10 minutes or until the Brussels sprouts are tender-crisp.

While the Brussels sprouts and carrots are cooking, whisk together the orange juice, maple syrup, miso and cornstarch in a small bowl. When the vegetables are tender-crisp, reduce the heat to medium-low and pour the mixture into the pan with the cooking vegetables, but don't stir. Cover and allow it to return to a simmer, then gently stir the sauce and vegetables. Cook for 4 minutes. The sauce should lightly coat the vegetables. Stir in the butter and ensure the vegetables are fully glazed. Season again with additional salt if desired. Sprinkle with toasted pecans just before serving.

GLUTEN-FREE OPTION Replace the miso with gluten-free miso.

PARSNIP, CAULIFLOWER AND POTATO MASH WITH SAGE

Potatoes, cauliflower and parsnip are mashed together with sage, nutmeg, ginger and a touch of soft goat cheese to give these mashed potatoes a different flair. Creamy, fragrant and full of flavour, this may forever change the way you make mashed potatoes. Serve them as a fluffy side or traditionally piped and baked into Duchess potatoes. If you are making them Duchess style, you can freeze them—and then bake them hot and golden just before you serve them. An impressive, quick and easy side-dish solution! This mash is lovely with the Maple Miso Glazed Brussels Sprouts and Carrots with Toasted Pecans (page 48).

Serves 4 **GF**

1½ cups (375 mL) red potatoes, peeled and diced into 1-inch (2.5 cm) cubes
1½ cups (375 mL) cauliflower florets
1 cup (250 mL) parsnip, peeled and diced into 1-inch (2.5 cm) cubes
2 Tbsp (30 mL) soft goat cheese
1½ tsp (7 mL) chopped fresh sage
Pinch of ground nutmeg
Pinch of ground ginger
Pinch of sea salt

TIP: This veggie mash tops the Steel-Cut Oat Shepherd's Pie with Parsnip, Cauliflower and Potato Mash with Sage. See page 165.

Place potatoes, cauliflower and parsnips together in a medium saucepan and cover with cold water. Cover and bring to a boil, then reduce heat and cook for about 7 to 10 minutes or until the vegetables are tender and easily pierced with a fork. Drain the water and add the goat cheese to the saucepan. Mash or purée with an immersion blender until smooth and creamy. Season with the sage, nutmeg, ginger and salt.

OPTIONS

Baked Duchess potatoes: Preheat the oven to broil, 550°F (290°C). Line a medium baking sheet with parchment paper and set aside. Place vegetable mash mixture into a piping bag (or a resealable plastic bag with a 1-inch/2.5 cm corner cut off). Pipe or scoop ¼ cup (60 mL) of mash into a round rosette onto the baking sheet. Bake for 4 to 6 minutes until edges are golden.

Make and freeze: Prepare the Duchess potatoes and place on a baking sheet that will fit in your freezer lined with waxed or parchment paper. Place the vegetable mash mixture into a piping bag (or a resealable plastic bag with a 1-inch/2.5 cm corner cut off). Pipe or scoop ¼ cup (60 mL) of mash into a round rosette on the baking sheet. Place in the freezer for 1 hour. Remove and individually wrap or place in a resealable freezer container or plastic bag. When ready to bake, unwrap, place on a parchment-lined baking sheet and broil at 550°F (290°C) for 12 to 15 minutes or until the edges are golden and the inside is piping hot.

ZA'ATAR DUSTED VEGGIE FRIES

These veggie fries are a colourful medley of root vegetables tossed with fragrant za'atar spice. They make for a unique side to any family dinner or an elegant and simple small plate. Try different combinations of your favourite vegetables, such as potatoes, celery root, parsnip, zucchini, sweet or red potato, turnip, carrot (purple, orange or yellow) and rutabaga. Just remember that sweet potatoes and zucchini tend to cook and soften faster, so you may want to add them 5 to 10 minutes later in the baking process. These delicious beauties are fabulous partners to the Guacamole Portobello Burgers with Miso Barbecue Sauce (page 138) or serve with Creamy Mayonnaise (page 197), Tomato Ketchup (page 196) or your favourite dip.

Serves 4 to 6 **DF**

8 medium red potatoes, peeled
   and sliced lengthwise into
   3- × ½-inch (8 × 1 cm) strips
4 large carrots, peeled and sliced
   lengthwise into 3- × ½-inch
   (8 × 1 cm) strips
2 large sweet potatoes, peeled and
   sliced lengthwise into 3- × ½-inch
   (8 × 1 cm) strips
1 medium turnip, peeled and sliced
   lengthwise into 3- × ½-inch
   (8 × 1 cm) strips
1 medium rutabaga, peeled and
   sliced lengthwise into 3- × ½-inch
   (8 × 1 cm) strips
1 Tbsp (15 mL) grapeseed oil
2 Tbsp (30 mL) za'atar (see Tip)
Sea salt, to taste
   (optional, see Tip)

Preheat the oven to 350°F (180°C). Line a large baking sheet with parchment paper and set aside.

Toss the sliced vegetables with the oil in a large bowl. Dust with the za'atar and salt (if using), and spread on the prepared baking sheet. Bake for 25 to 30 minutes or until the edges are crispy and golden.

> TIP: Za'atar is a Middle Eastern blend of fragrant spices most often containing sumac, thyme, marjoram, roasted sesame seeds, oregano and sometimes salt. If the blend you purchase does not contain salt, you can add it in this recipe. You can also make your own za'atar with ½ cup (125 mL) ground sumac, 1 Tbsp (15 mL) each of dried thyme, dried marjoram and dried oregano, 2 tsp (10 mL) roasted sesame seeds and ½ tsp (2 mL) kosher salt.

CRISPY BAKED ONION RINGS
WITH TANGY DIPPING SAUCE

If you're going to take the time to make onion rings, you want them to be delicious! Full of flavour, these onion rings don't last long at our house and won't last long at yours, especially when served with this tasty tangy dipping sauce. If you're gluten-free, feel free to use rice flour and gluten-free croutons to coat the rings. Serve these alongside the Pepper-Crusted Mushroom Steaks (page 160) or the Hot Barbecue Veggie and Superslaw Sandwiches (page 137).

Serves 4 to 8

TANGY DIPPING SAUCE
½ cup (125 mL) sour cream
2 Tbsp (30 mL) seafood sauce
¼ tsp (1 mL) dried oregano
Pinch of garlic salt
Pinch of black pepper
Pinch of cayenne pepper (optional)

CRISPY BAKED ONION RINGS
1 large (about 1 lb/450 g) sweet
   yellow onion, cut into slices
   ½ inch (1 cm) thick
1½ cups (375 mL) all-purpose flour
2 large eggs
2 Tbsp (30 mL) milk
1½ cups (375 mL) crushed Crisp
   and Smoky Croutons (page 204)
   or store-bought Caesar salad
   croutons
½ tsp (2 mL) seasoning salt

Prepare the sauce by mixing the sour cream, seafood sauce, oregano, garlic salt, black pepper and cayenne (if using) in a small bowl. Chill, covered, in the refrigerator until ready to use.

Preheat the oven to 450°F (230°C). Line one large or two small baking sheets with parchment paper and set aside. Separate the onion into rings and place on a plate or in a bowl. Place the flour in a shallow bowl and set aside. Whisk the egg and the milk together in a separate shallow bowl and set aside. Mix the crushed croutons and seasoning salt in a large resealable bag and set aside.

Place the items on your work surface in the following order: onion bowl or plate, flour bowl, egg mixture bowl and bag of crumb mixture. Place the baking sheet after the crumb mixture.

It's important to reserve one hand for the dry work and the other for the wet work to prevent a grand mess (left hand dry, right hand wet, or reversed for lefties). Place one onion ring in the flour mixture and coat. Then coat in the egg mixture, turning with a fork. Toss and coat the ring in crumbs and place on the baking tray. Repeat with the remaining onion rings. If needed, place some of the smaller rings inside the larger ones with about 1 inch (2.5 cm) of space between them.

Bake for 8 minutes on each side or until tender and golden. Place on a serving tray and serve with dipping sauce.

ROASTED ROOT VEGETABLES WITH MISO, GINGER AND MAPLE

These slices of daikon, carrot and beet are gently roasted with maple, fresh ginger and a hint of miso to create a warm side dish that is full of nutrition, colour and flavour. Serve this side with sandwiches, wraps or burgers, such as the Grilled Pineapple Teriyaki Burgers (page 140), Cheesy Veggie Joes (page 139) or Guacamole Portobello Burgers with Miso Barbecue Sauce (page 138).

Serves 6

2 cups (500 mL) peeled and
    sliced daikon
2 cups (500 mL) peeled and
    sliced golden or red beets
2 cups (500 mL) peeled and
    sliced carrot
2 Tbsp (30 mL) pure maple syrup
2 Tbsp (30 mL) fresh orange juice
1 tsp (5 mL) red miso
1 tsp (5 mL) grated fresh ginger

Preheat the oven to 375°F (190°C). Place the sliced daikon, beets and carrot in an 11- × 7-inch (2 L) baking dish and set aside.

In a small jar, combine the maple syrup, juice, miso and ginger and shake well. Pour half of the mixture over the vegetables in the baking dish, and reserve the rest.

Roast the vegetables in the oven for 30 minutes. Drizzle the remaining half of the maple syrup mixture over the roasted vegetables and serve.

GLUTEN-FREE OPTION Replace the miso with gluten-free miso.

CHIPOTLE REFRIED BEANS

These smoky refried beans are made from the Maple and Sumac Baked Beans (page 148). Blended together with chipotle peppers in adobo sauce, vegetable broth and a touch of fresh cilantro, these beans make a hearty burrito, salad or nacho topping or even a zesty dip for crudité or tortilla chips. If you want even more of that spicy kick, just add more chipotle peppers to your blend. Try these beans alongside the Fire Roasted Salsa with Home Baked Tortilla Chips (page 33) or the Whole Wheat Soft Flour Tortillas (page 117).

Serves 4 to 6

2 cups (500 mL) Maple and Sumac Baked Beans (page 148)
½ cup (125 mL) Simple Vegetable Broth (page 62) or low-sodium, store-bought vegetable broth
1 Tbsp (15 mL) chipotle peppers in adobo sauce
¼ cup (60 mL) chopped fresh cilantro

Place the baked beans in a food processor or high-speed blender and purée, adding the broth to thin the mixture and ensure it blends smoothly. Add the peppers and cilantro, and continue to process mixture until well blended and smooth.

Place the mixture in a medium saucepan over medium-low heat, and cook until heated through. Serve warm.

GLUTEN-FREE OPTION When making the Maple and Sumac Baked Beans (page 148), use gluten-free Worcestershire sauce.

CARIBBEAN COCONUT AND BLACK BEAN QUINOA

This creamy coconut and black bean quinoa is taken to the next level with the addition of fresh thyme and a hint of heat. It pairs perfectly with the Jamaican Jerk Tofu (page 149) and Superslaw (page 104) for a fabulous summer dinner.

Serves 4 to 6 DF GF V

1 Tbsp (15 mL) vegetable oil
½ cup (125 mL) diced onion
2 cloves garlic, minced
1 Thai red chili pepper, minced
1 cup (250 mL) quinoa
1½ cups (375 mL) Simple Vegetable
   Broth (page 62) or low-sodium,
   store-bought vegetable broth
1 can (14 oz/398 mL) full-fat
   coconut milk
1 cup (250 mL) cooked black beans
2 tsp (10 mL) fresh thyme leaves
¼ tsp (1 mL) sea salt (optional)

Preheat the oil in a large saucepan on medium-low heat. Add the onion, stirring occasionally for 2 minutes. Add the garlic, chili pepper and quinoa, and stir until hot. Pour in the broth and 1 cup (250 mL) of the coconut milk, and bring to a simmer. Cover and reduce to medium-low heat. Cook for 10 minutes.

Stir in the beans, the remaining coconut milk, the thyme and salt (if using). Cover, return to a simmer and then turn the heat off. Let sit covered on the burner for another 10 minutes. Serve.

SOUPS, STEWS AND CHILIES

SIMPLE MUSHROOM BROTH

Mushroom broth can be a key ingredient in soups, stews, gravies, chilies and noodle dishes, and can provide that perfect flavour hit you're looking for. We recommend cremini, shiitake, porcini and chanterelle for their stronger flavours, but all mushrooms will work, even simple white button mushrooms! So use whatever is available and meets your budget. Many varieties of dried mushrooms are available in large bags at fair prices from Asian grocery stores. Freeze prepared broth in labelled, premeasured serving sizes for easy use at a later date.

Makes 14 cups (3.5 L)   DF GF V

4 cups (1 L) dried mushrooms
　(3½ oz/100 g)
1 medium onion, halved, skin on
2 to 3 sprigs of fresh parsley
1 rosemary sprig
2 cloves garlic
16 cups (4 L) water
Sea salt and pepper, to taste

Place mushrooms, onion, parsley, rosemary, garlic and water in a large (6 quart/6 L) stockpot over medium-high heat. Bring to a boil and then reduce to a simmer. Simmer for 1 to 2 hours, or longer, until desired mushroom flavour is achieved.

Remove and discard mushrooms, onion, garlic cloves and herb sprigs from the pot using a slotted spoon. The mushrooms will be fully saturated and will have sunk to the bottom of the pot. Strain the broth into a large bowl or saucepan. You may have to strain it multiple times to remove all mushroom bits. Use a paper coffee filter or paper-towel-lined strainer to remove any remaining fine sediment. Season with salt and pepper. Divide into 1-cup (250 mL) servings, and place in resealable freezer containers for future use.

SIMPLE VEGETABLE BROTH

A basic vegetable broth is so easy to make! When our grandma made broth, it was a big pot of messy, barely washed vegetables and skins boiled in water. Nothing has changed! All you need are your favourite vegetables or vegetable scraps, herbs and a large pot of water, and voila! Just remember to use salt and seasonings sparingly (including garlic) when you prepare the broth. You may have many different uses for the broth, so keeping it mild will allow for more flexibility later when you use it in various recipes.

Makes 12 to 14 cups (3 to 3.5 L) **DF** **GF** **V**

1 small rutabaga, halved (if the skin is waxed, remove the skin)
1 small celeriac, skin removed and halved
1 bunch of leek greens (no whites)
2 to 3 carrots, unpeeled
2 to 3 parsnips, unpeeled
2 to 3 celery stalks
1 medium onion, halved, skin on
1 apple, halved, unpeeled, with core
2 to 3 sprigs of fresh parsley
1 rosemary sprig
2 bay leaves
1 to 2 cloves garlic
3 to 4 juniper berries (optional)
16 cups (4 L) water
Sea salt, to taste (optional)

Place the rutabaga, celeriac, leeks, carrots, parsnips, celery, onion, apple, parsley, rosemary, bay leaves, garlic and juniper berries (if using) in a large (6 quart/6 L) stockpot. Add the water, ensuring all the vegetables are covered. At medium to high heat, bring to a boil and then reduce to a simmer. Simmer for 1 to 2 hours until desired vegetable flavour is achieved.

Remove and discard the large vegetables from the pot using a slotted spoon. Strain the broth into a large bowl or saucepan. You may have to strain it multiple times to remove all the solids. Season with salt (if using) or wait to season when you use it in recipes. We like to add just a touch of salt at this stage, not more than ¼ tsp (1 mL). Divide into 1-cup (250 mL) servings, and place in resealable freezer containers for future use.

TIP: Plenty of other vegetables make great broth! Try adding mushrooms, more apples, root vegetables, squash and various herbs. Collect scraps of raw vegetables (yes! scraps, including carrot tops, mushroom stems, peels and vegetable trimmings) and freeze them until you have enough to make broth.

CANTALOUPE CITRUS GAZPACHO

A summer must-have, gazpacho is delicious and refreshing—and certainly a time-saver. Keep a cool jug of it in your refrigerator for a week at a time, ready to eat whenever you need a speedy starter or side for lunch or dinner. Be creative and serve it in something unusual, like ramekins, shot glasses or even egg cups. Serve this soup with the Ripe Peach and Pistachio Butter Lettuce Wraps (page 120) or the Crisp Iceberg Wedge Salad with Cashews and Chili Mango Dressing (page 93).

Serves 4

3 cups (750 mL) peeled and
  chopped cantaloupe
1 cup (250 mL) peeled and
  chopped orange
1 Tbsp (15 mL) chopped
  fresh ginger
1 Tbsp (15 mL) fresh lime juice
1 tsp (5 mL) fresh lime zest
¼ cup (60 mL) plain 6% Greek yogurt
1 tsp (5 mL) chopped fresh cilantro

Place the cantaloupe, orange, ginger, lime juice and zest in a blender or food processor, and purée until smooth. Chill for at least an hour. Divide into bowls and top each with 1 Tbsp (15 mL) of yogurt and a tiny pinch of cilantro. Serve.

RAW OPTION Replace the Greek yogurt with raw yogurt.

> TIP: Try adding a sprinkle of the savoury Dulse Bacon Bits (page 203) on top!

MUSHROOM RED CHARD SOUP

This is a soothing, brothy soup with chunks of meaty mushrooms and earthy, red chard. Serve a steaming bowl of this along with a buttered slab of your favourite seedy bread. A wonderful meal on a cold autumn or winter day!

Serves 2

1 tsp (5 mL) grapeseed oil
1 cup (250 mL) chopped
  white onion
1 tsp (5 mL) minced garlic
1 tsp (5 mL) sea salt
½ cup (125 mL) dried porcini
  mushrooms, rehydrated in ½ cup
  (125 mL) water
½ cup (125 mL) chopped
  cremini mushrooms
3½ cups (875 mL) Simple Vegetable
  Broth (page 62) or low-sodium,
  store-bought vegetable broth
6 to 12 sprigs of fresh thyme
1 cup (250 mL) chopped red chard
  (or green)
2 tsp (10 mL) apple cider vinegar
2 tsp (10 mL) soy sauce
Ground black pepper, to taste
  (optional)

In a large saucepan, place the oil and onion and sauté until translucent. Add the garlic, salt and mushrooms (save the rehydration juice), and continue to sauté for 3 to 4 minutes or until fragrant.

Add the broth, mushroom juice and thyme sprigs, and bring to a boil. Reduce to a simmer and add the chard, vinegar and soy sauce. Simmer for 8 to 10 minutes or until soup tastes flavourful. Discard the thyme sprigs. Season with additional salt and pepper if desired.

GLUTEN-FREE OPTION Replace the soy sauce with gluten-free tamari.

HOT BOK CHOY AND SHIITAKE MUSHROOM SOUP WITH BLACK GARLIC

A nice change from the everyday. Create the perfect balance of flavour with fresh vegetables enhanced with a little heat, along with the unique taste of black garlic. Black garlic is fermented garlic that takes on mild and sweet flavours with that slight tang of fermentation. The wonderfully rich and savoury umami notes to this dish easily make you forget it's meatless. The Vegetable Nori Wraps with Orange Ginger Miso Dressing (page 37) would pair perfectly as an appetizer for this soup.

Serves 4 **DF**

4 large eggs
2½ oz (70 g) rice vermicelli noodles
4 cups (1 L) Simple Vegetable Broth (page 62) or low-sodium, store-bought vegetable broth
3½ oz (100 g) shiitake mushrooms, quartered if large
1-inch (2.5 cm) piece of fresh ginger, peeled and sliced into ¼-inch (5 mm) pieces
2 mini bok choy, halved lengthwise
1½ tsp (7 mL) soy sauce
1½ tsp (7 mL) toasted sesame oil
2 tsp (10 mL) rice vinegar
2 green onions, thinly sliced
3 cloves black garlic, minced
Thinly sliced Thai red chili pepper or Sriracha hot sauce, to taste

Bring 3 cups (750 mL) of water to a boil in a small saucepan over high heat. Use a slotted spoon to carefully place the whole eggs (in their shells) into the water. Cook for 7 to 8 minutes or until semi-soft. Remove the eggs with a slotted spoon and immerse them in cold water. Peel the eggs when they are cool to the touch. Halve lengthwise and set aside.

Bring 4 cups (1 L) of water to a boil in a medium saucepan over high heat. Cook the rice noodles for about 5 minutes or until just tender. Place the noodles in a fine mesh strainer and rinse with cold water. Set aside.

Bring the broth, mushrooms and ginger to a simmer in a medium saucepan. Cover and cook for about 10 minutes. Add the bok choy, soy sauce and oil. Cover and simmer for another 5 minutes. Stir in the vinegar.

Run hot water over the noodles before serving. Place some noodles in the bottom of each bowl. Ladle soup over the noodles. Garnish with the green onions, egg halves and black garlic. Enjoy with your choice of chili pepper or hot sauce if desired.

GLUTEN-FREE OPTION Replace the soy sauce with gluten-free tamari.

MISO VEGETABLE BORSCHT

Miso gives this soup the full-flavour enhancement that a meat-based broth would normally provide. Freeze any extras or double the recipe for additional freezer meals. We add the miso at the end of cooking to protect the integrity of its nutrition and prevent the flavour from becoming bitter. This soup would pair nicely with a salad or flatbread. Try it with the Five-Minute Cucumber and Herb Salad (page 89) or the Roasted Tomato, Garlic, Arugula and Goat Cheese Flatbread (page 121).

Serves 4 to 6

1 Tbsp (15 mL) grapeseed oil
　or vegetable oil
⅓ cup (75 mL) diced
　yellow onion
½ cup (125 mL) grated carrot
¼ tsp (1 mL) sea salt
¼ tsp (1 mL) minced garlic
1½ tsp (7 mL) tomato paste
1½ cups (375 mL) shredded green
　cabbage
1½ cups (375 mL) grated red beets
4 cups (1 L) Simple Vegetable Broth
　(page 62) or low-sodium, store-
　bought vegetable broth
1½ tsp (7 mL) fresh lemon juice
3 Tbsp (45 mL) chopped fresh dill
1 Tbsp (15 mL) red miso
½ cup (125 mL) water
¼ cup (60 mL) sour cream,
　to garnish
4 to 6 sprigs of fresh dill,
　to garnish

Heat a large saucepan with the oil on low heat. Add the onion, carrot and salt. Cook, covered, until the onion is tender, about 5 to 7 minutes. Stir in the garlic and heat for 20 to 30 seconds. Stir in the tomato paste until evenly distributed. Add the cabbage, beets, broth, lemon juice and dill. Bring to a simmer over medium-low heat, then cover for 30 minutes or until the vegetables are tender.

In a measuring cup, stir the miso into the water until dispersed and no lumps remain (there will be small bits of soy but no large lumps). Pour into the saucepan and heat until hot but not boiling. Ladle the soup into bowls and serve with a spoonful of sour cream and small sprig of dill on top. The soup can be frozen in resealable containers, if desired. Thaw in the refrigerator overnight and gently reheat.

GLUTEN-FREE OPTION Replace the miso with gluten-free miso.

ROASTED CAULIFLOWER SOUP
WITH TARRAGON BROWN BUTTER

This is a wonderfully velvety soup that is rich with the flavours of roasted cauliflower and garlic. Blended smooth, you may think this is a cream soup, but don't be fooled, it's all vegetable! The luxurious texture and complex flavour are further accented with a crowning swirl of warm, herbed tarragon brown butter.

Serves 4 **GF**

1 large head cauliflower,
    florets trimmed
2 to 4 cloves garlic, skin on
1 Tbsp (15 mL) grapeseed oil
1 cup (250 mL) finely
    chopped onion
2 Tbsp (30 mL) liquid honey
4 to 5 sprigs of fresh tarragon
4 to 5 sprigs of fresh parsley
4 cups (1 L) Simple Vegetable Broth
    (page 62) or low-sodium, store-
    bought vegetable broth
¼ cup (60 mL) salted butter
¾ tsp (3 mL) sea salt
¼ tsp (1 mL) ground black pepper

> TIP: Add more complex flavour to this brown butter soup by adding a few dried red chilies when you add the bouquet garni, or top the finished soup with croutons (gluten-free, if required), a swirl of yogurt or sour cream or even a small sprinkle of lemon zest.

Preheat the oven to 425°F (220°C) and line a large baking sheet with parchment paper. Place cauliflower florets and garlic cloves on pan and roast for 17 to 20 minutes, stirring halfway through to ensure the florets are evenly light brown. Remove from the oven and set aside.

Place the oil and onion in a large saucepan or stockpot, and sauté on medium-low heat until translucent and the edges are brown. Peel and mince the roasted garlic cloves and add them to the saucepan. Add the honey and the roasted cauliflower and stir. Make a bouquet garni with 3 to 4 of the tarragon sprigs and all of the parsley sprigs by tying them together with a piece of non-waxed kitchen string. Reserve one tarragon sprig for later. Add the broth and the bouquet garni to the saucepan, and simmer for 25 to 30 minutes.

Meanwhile, place the butter in a shallow pan with a light-coloured bottom (stainless steel, not black or non-stick). (The pan needs to be light so you will easily see the butter browning and not burn it). Place over medium heat, stirring the butter constantly as it melts and foams. Add the remaining tarragon sprig. As the butter cooks, small, very fine brown specks will form. After a few minutes, the butter will be browned. Remove it from the heat quickly (burning will change the flavour). Discard tarragon sprig. Set the brown butter aside.

Remove the soup from the heat and purée in a blender (in 2 batches if necessary) or by using an immersion blender until smooth. Reheat if necessary. Add the salt and pepper, and stir. Divide into 4 servings and top each with 1 Tbsp (15 mL) of brown butter drizzle. Serve immediately.

VEGAN OPTION Replace the honey with pure maple syrup and omit the brown butter.

ROASTED BUTTERNUT SQUASH AND APPLE SOUP WITH CRISP AND SMOKY CROUTONS

Life is good when you sit down to a homemade bowl of hot soup. It satisfies the soul just like fresh mountain air or a good book. Enjoy the sweet and smoky flavours of this soup, topped with a dollop of sour cream and savoury, crunchy croutons. A little piece of heaven without leaving your kitchen. Even better, this dish is the perfect candidate for a make-ahead meal. Freeze this soup and reheat gently on a day when you're short on time.

Serves 6 to 8

1½ lbs (680 g) butternut squash, halved lengthwise and seeded
2 Tbsp (30 mL) grapeseed oil
¾ cup (175 mL) chopped celery
¾ cup (175 mL) peeled and chopped carrot
¾ cup (175 mL) chopped yellow onion
1 tsp (5 mL) sea salt
1 tsp (5 mL) minced garlic
½ tsp (2 mL) smoked paprika
¼ tsp (1 mL) ground cumin
¼ tsp (1 mL) ground coriander
1½ cups (375 mL) peeled and chopped sweet potato (about ¾ lb/340 g)
2 medium Granny Smith apples, peeled and chopped (about ¾ lb/340 g)
4 cups (1 L) Simple Vegetable Broth (page 62) or low-sodium, store-bought vegetable broth
½ cup (125 mL) water
½ cup (125 mL) sour cream
½ cup (125 mL) Crisp and Smoky Croutons (page 204)
2 tsp (10 mL) fresh chopped cilantro, to garnish (optional)

Preheat the oven to 375°F (190°C). Line a baking dish with parchment paper, and place the butternut squash cut side down. Adding 1 Tbsp (15 mL) of water to the dish. Bake for 40 minutes or until a knife can be easily inserted through the thickest part of the squash. Remove from the oven and let cool. Scoop out the flesh after it has cooled enough to handle.

Heat the oil in a large saucepan over medium-low heat. Stir in the celery, carrot, onion and salt. Cook for about 7 minutes or until tender. Stir in the garlic, paprika, cumin and coriander and heat for 30 seconds. Add the cooked squash and the sweet potato, apples, broth and water. Bring to a simmer, cover and cook on low for about 30 minutes or until the vegetables are tender.

Purée soup with an immersion blender or in small batches in a blender. Add a small amount of water if necessary to reach the desired consistency. Return the soup to the saucepan and reheat. Ladle into bowls and top each with a dollop of sour cream and a few croutons. Garnish with cilantro (if using).

TIP: Want to cook the squash on the barbecue? Preheat the barbecue to around 375°F (190°C). Lightly oil the squash and place cut side down on a small parchment-lined baking sheet. Cook for 30 minutes and check every 5 additional minutes for doneness. Lightly scrape any dark areas and use the squash in recipe as directed. You can also cook squash in a slow cooker. Add 2 Tbsp (30 mL) of water and cook on low for 8 hours, until tender.

IMMUNE BOOST MASON JAR SOUP

A combination of East Asian ingredients—lemongrass, ginger, garlic and chili pepper—are thought to improve immunity. So when you feel like you need to recharge or you're under the weather, we'd recommend this to anyone as the perfect nutritionally powerful soup. Even better, it's quick and easy to prepare. This soup's components can be placed in a mason jar, stored and used when you need a restorative, warm meal.

Serves 1

1 oz (30 g) rice vermicelli noodles
½-inch (1 cm) piece of fresh
  lemongrass, thinly sliced
1-inch (2.5 cm) piece of fresh ginger,
  peeled and halved
1 large or 2 small fresh basil leaves,
  chiffonade (see Tip on page 102)
1 Thai chili pepper, halved
  lengthwise, seeds removed
½ tsp (2 mL) dry vegetable bouillon
  (or half of a 5 g cube)
¼ tsp (1 tsp) minced garlic
¼ to ½ tsp (1 to 2 mL) liquid honey
¼ tsp (1 tsp) fresh lime zest
1 lime wedge

Place the noodles, lemongrass, ginger, basil, chili pepper, bouillon, garlic, honey, lime zest and lime wedge in a 2-cup (500 mL) mason jar. Tighten the lid and place in the refrigerator for up to 1 day.

When you are ready to make the soup, remove the lime wedge and pour in 1½ cups (375 mL) of boiling water. Gently seal the lid and let sit for 7 minutes or until the noodles are tender. Remove the ginger and pepper pieces. Squeeze the lime into the soup and eat immediately.

VEGAN OPTION Replace the honey with pure maple syrup.

CHARRED TOMATO AND ASPARAGUS SOUP WITH SOFT GOAT CHEESE CRUMBLES

Enjoy a comforting bowl of vegetable goodness in under 30 minutes. The amped-up, smoky flavour of roasted tomato adds richness without extra calories and crisp tender asparagus accented with creamy goat cheese make for a light but luxurious meal. Still hungry? Add the Red Pepper and Black Olive Cauliflower Pizza (page 129), or eat it with your favourite grilled cheese sandwich.

Serves 4 to 6

2 Tbsp (30 mL) unsalted butter
⅔ cup (150 mL) diced yellow onion
½ tsp (2 mL) minced garlic
¼ tsp (1 mL) red pepper flakes
2 cans (each 14 oz/398 mL) fire-roasted tomatoes, whole or diced
2 cups (500 mL) Simple Vegetable Broth (page 62) or low-sodium, store-bought vegetable broth
½ lb (225 g) asparagus, tough ends trimmed, cut into ½-inch (1 cm) lengths
⅔ cup (150 mL) half-and-half cream
¼ tsp (1 mL) ground black pepper
¼ to ⅓ cup (60 to 75 mL) crumbled soft, unripened goat cheese
1 to 1½ Tbsp (15 to 22 mL) minced fresh chives

Heat a large saucepan on medium-low heat and add the butter. Add the onion, cover and cook for 5 minutes or until the onion begins to soften. Stir in the garlic and red pepper flakes and heat for 1 minute. Add the roasted tomatoes and broth. Purée with an immersion blender or in a blender (in small batches if necessary) until smooth.

Bring the soup to a simmer over medium-low heat. Add the asparagus, cover and cook for 5 to 7 minutes or until the asparagus is tender-crisp. Stir in the cream and pepper and gently reheat until hot. Ladle into bowls. Top with crumbled goat cheese and chives.

MIGHTY MEDITERRANEAN MINESTRONE

Our version of this classic soup is chock-full of vegetables, creating a mighty dose of flavour and nutrition! Although you can make this any time of year, there is no doubt a warm bowl of this hearty minestrone and a piece of crusty bread tastes even better when cooler weather has arrived. This soup is the perfect accompaniment to the Roasted Tomato, Garlic, Arugula and Goat Cheese Flatbread (page 121) or the Open-Faced Artichoke and Mushroom BLT (page 134).

Serves 6 to 8   **DF** **GF** **V**

2 Tbsp (30 mL) grapeseed oil or
   vegetable oil
1 cup (250 mL) chopped
   yellow onion
1 cup (250 mL) chopped carrot
1 cup (250 mL) diced celery
¾ tsp (3 mL) sea salt
¼ tsp (1 mL) ground black pepper
1½ tsp (7 mL) minced garlic
1 can (19 oz/540 mL) six bean blend,
   drained and rinsed
1 can (14 oz/398 mL) diced tomatoes
4 cups (1 L) Simple Vegetable Broth
   (page 62) or low-sodium, store-
   bought vegetable broth
1 tsp (5 mL) dried parsley
¼ tsp (1 mL) dried thyme
1 cup (250 mL) green beans,
   trimmed and cut in
   1-inch (2.5 cm) pieces
1 Tbsp (15 mL) cornstarch
¼ cup (60 mL) cool water
Pinch of smoked paprika

Heat a large saucepan over medium-low heat. Add the oil, onion, carrot, celery, salt and pepper. Cover and cook for 5 to 7 minutes or until the celery and onion start to soften. Stir in the garlic and heat for another 30 seconds.

Add the beans, tomatoes (including the liquid), broth, parsley and thyme, and bring to a simmer. Cover and cook for 15 minutes.

Add the green beans. Whisk the cornstarch with the water in a small bowl. Stir into the soup and bring back to a simmer until the green beans and other vegetables are tender. Season with the paprika and serve.

SLOW COOKER FRENCH ONION MISO SOUP

Need an easy soup that tastes like a timeless old-favourite, without all the work? Try this easy French onion soup made in a slow cooker and have homemade soup for an effortless weekday supper. Savoury miso acts as a key ingredient in this recipe as it replaces the umami flavour that beef broth would normally provide. Freeze extras (without the baguette and cheese) for an even quicker meal when you need it. This yummy soup is great served alongside the Tossed Baby Arugula and Zucchini Salad (page 90), the Lazy Layered Salad (page 102) or the Microgreen and Fig Salad with Hemp Seed Gremolata (page 96).

Serves 8

2 Tbsp (30 mL) salted butter
1 Tbsp (15 mL) grapeseed oil
4 lbs (1.8 kg) large yellow or sweet onion, halved and thinly sliced
2 tsp (10 mL) minced garlic
1 tsp (5 mL) sea salt
¼ cup (60 mL) dry sherry
6 cups (1.5 L) Simple Vegetable Broth (page 62) or low-sodium, store-bought vegetable broth, reserve ½ cup (125 mL)
2 Tbsp (30 mL) yellow or red miso
2 Tbsp (30 mL) all-purpose flour
8 slices of baguette or 16 demi-baguette slices, toasted
1½ cups (375 mL) shredded mozzarella and/or Swiss cheese
Freshly ground black pepper, to taste

Set the slow cooker to the low temperature setting. Add the butter, oil, sliced onion, garlic and salt. Cook on low for 6 to 8 hours or until the onion is golden and tender. Stir occasionally if desired, but it isn't necessary.

Turn the heat setting to high and stir in the sherry. Heat 5½ cups (1.37 L) of the broth in a large saucepan until boiling. (Heating the broth separately speeds up the preparation. Adding it directly to the slow cooker unheated would require additional time waiting for the broth to heat up.) Pour the hot broth into the slow cooker. Whisk the miso and flour into the reserved ½ cup (125 mL) of cool broth until no lumps remain. Gently add, whisking into the slow cooker. Cover and allow to heat for 10 to 15 minutes or until slightly thickened.

Preheat the oven broiler. Place 8 ovenproof bowls on a baking sheet. Ladle soup into each of the bowls. Place toasted baguette slices on top, followed by approximately 3 Tbsp (45 mL) of mozzarella cheese on each baguette slice. Place under the broiler for 1 to 2 minutes or until the cheese is bubbly and golden. Serve with black pepper if desired.

GLUTEN-FREE OPTION Replace the miso with gluten-free miso, the all-purpose flour with rice flour and use gluten-free baguettes.

RUSTIC FARMHOUSE SOUP

You can prepare a hearty bowl of split pea and barley vegetable soup with ingredients you likely have in your refrigerator and cupboard. A versatile soup, this recipe lends itself well to replacing the barley with an equal measurement of other grains. We recommend quinoa or sorghum, which are both fantastic gluten-free options. Freeze any leftovers for a healthy, last-minute meal. This soup is a delicious starter to the Warm Cauliflower and Chickpea Mixed Green Salad with White Balsamic Vinaigrette (page 111).

Serves 6 to 8

1 Tbsp (15 mL) grapeseed oil
1 cup (250 mL) chopped onion
1 cup (250 mL) chopped celery
1 cup (250 mL) chopped carrot
¾ cup (175 mL) yellow split peas, sorted and rinsed
¾ cup (175 mL) pearl barley
1 tsp (5 mL) minced garlic
¼ tsp (1 mL) poultry seasoning
1½ tsp (7 mL) sea salt
¼ tsp (1 mL) ground black pepper
4 cups (1 L) Simple Vegetable Broth (page 62) or low-sodium, store-bought vegetable broth
4 cups (1 L) water
1 Tbsp (15 mL) minced fresh parsley

In a slow cooker: Heat a large saucepan over medium-low heat. Add the oil, onion, celery and carrot, and cook until the onion and celery are starting to soften. Place the onion, celery and carrot mixture along with the split peas, barley, garlic, poultry seasoning, salt and pepper in the slow cooker and stir. Add the broth and water. Cook in the slow cooker for 8 hours on low or 4 to 6 hours on high.

When the split peas are tender and vegetables are fully cooked, stir in the parsley. Season again with additional salt and pepper if desired and serve.

On the stovetop: Heat a large saucepan over medium-low heat. Add the oil, onion, celery and carrot, and cook until the onion and celery are starting to soften. Add the split peas, barley, garlic, poultry seasoning, salt and pepper. Add the broth and water. Simmer on low for 3 hours until split peas are tender.

When the split peas are tender and vegetables are fully cooked, stir in the parsley. Season again with additional salt and pepper if desired and serve.

GLUTEN-FREE OPTION Replace the barley with sorghum or quinoa.

> TIP: Sorting split peas is necessary to remove any misshapen peas, small stones or plant matter that has not been winnowed away when it was packaged.

EFFORTLESS NINE BEAN SALSA
SLOW COOKER SOUP WITH AVOCADO

We love the freshness of the tomato and avocado in this soup, in combination with the richness of the salsa and beans. This recipe is not only flavourful but also incredibly handy for the days when minutes are all you can spare for dinner prep. The only thing you will need to plan ahead will be soaking the beans the night before. To extend the servings and make it heartier, this soup is wonderful served over your favourite ancient grain or rice.

Serves 4 to 6   (V)

1½ cups (375 mL) dried nine-bean mix, sorted and rinsed

4 cups (1 L) Simple Vegetable Broth (page 62) or low-sodium, store-bought vegetable broth

2 cups (500 mL) water

2 cups (500 mL) chunky tomato salsa

1 cup (250 mL) frozen corn kernels

1 large tomato, diced

1 avocado, peeled, pitted and chopped

½ cup (125 mL) shredded Cheddar cheese (optional)

Soak the beans overnight in 5 cups (1.25 L) of cold water. Rinse the beans the next morning and place in a large 7-quart (7 L) slow cooker with the broth, water, salsa and corn. Cover and cook on low for 7 to 8 hours or until the beans are tender.

Stir in the tomato and ladle into bowls. Garnish with avocado and Cheddar cheese (if using). Serve immediately.

> TIP: Freeze leftovers (without the avocado and cheese) for up to 1½ months, and gently reheat and garnish as desired.

CHUNKY PUMPKIN VEGETABLE STEW

This earthy, sage-scented soup is filled with comforting chunks of pumpkin and potatoes, corn and red pepper. The heartiness is balanced by the velvety texture you create when you blend a portion of the cooked vegetables—a great trick to gain creaminess without adding any dairy. This is one of those soups that you'll quickly add to the top of your list of favourites!

Serves 6 DF GF V

1 to 2 Tbsp (5 to 10 mL) grapeseed oil or vegetable oil

½ cup (125 mL) chopped yellow onion

2 cups (500 mL) pumpkin, peeled and diced into ¾-inch (2 cm) cubes

1½ cups (375 mL) yellow potatoes, diced into ¾-inch (2 cm) cubes

1 cup (250 mL) diced sweet red pepper

1 cup (250 mL) canned fava beans, drained and rinsed

¾ cup (175 mL) frozen (thawed) or fresh corn kernels

4 cups (1 L) Simple Vegetable Broth (page 62) or low-sodium, store-bought vegetable broth

1 cup (250 mL) water

1 sage leaf

1 Tbsp (15 mL) chopped fresh parsley

½ tsp (2 mL) sea salt

Pinch of ground black pepper

2 Tbsp (30 mL) raw pepitas

6 fresh whole sage leaves, to garnish (optional)

In a large saucepan, place the oil and onion, and sauté until the onion is translucent and the edges are starting to brown. Add the pumpkin, potatoes, red pepper, beans and corn, and continue to sauté for 5 to 6 minutes or until vegetables begin to soften.

Add the broth, water and sage leaf, and bring to a boil. Reduce heat to a simmer and cook for 8 to 10 minutes or until the pumpkin and potatoes are just tender when pierced with a fork. Discard the sage leaf.

Remove 4 cups (1 L) of the soup's cooked vegetables (mostly pumpkin and potatoes) and place in a food processor or blender. Purée until smooth and then add this mixture back to the chunky soup. Stir well and season with parsley, salt and pepper. Ladle into bowls, and sprinkle each serving with pepitas. Garnish each bowl with a sage leaf (if using). Store any leftovers in the freezer for up to 4 weeks.

ANCHO TEMPEH CHILI

Even if you don't eat tofu often (or ever), you will be delighted by the meatless possibilities of tempeh. You'll have to make a point of bragging about the tempeh (or keeping it a secret) in this dish—depending on your audience—since it's not noticeably different from the texture of ground meat.

Serves 8

1 cup (250 mL) dry red kidney beans

1 cup (250 mL) dry black-eyed peas, navy beans or black beans

1 Tbsp (15 mL) grapeseed oil or vegetable oil

1 cup (250 mL) chopped white onion

2 tsp (10 mL) minced garlic

2 cups (500 mL) ground tempeh (ground in a food processor from an 8 oz/230 g vacuum-packed block)

2 cups (500 mL) Simple Vegetable Broth (page 62) or Simple Mushroom Broth (page 61) or low-sodium, store-bought vegetable broth

4 large dried, whole ancho chili peppers, stems and seeds removed

2 cups (500 mL) tomato sauce

1 cup (250 mL) hot coffee

¼ cup (60 mL) brown sugar

2 Tbsp (30 mL) unsweetened cocoa powder

2 tsp (10 mL) dried oregano

¾ tsp (3 mL) sea salt

½ tsp (2 mL) red pepper flakes

¼ tsp (1 mL) ground coriander

¼ tsp (1 mL) ground cumin

¼ tsp (1 mL) cayenne pepper

½ cup (125 mL) shredded aged white Cheddar cheese

Slices of avocado (optional)

Place the dried beans and peas in a large bowl and add enough water to cover. Refrigerate and soak the beans overnight.

Remove the beans and peas from the refrigerator, rinse and set aside. Place the oil and onion in a large saucepan over medium-high heat, and cook for 2 to 3 minutes, until the onion begins to soften. Add the garlic and ground tempeh. Continue to sauté for 5 to 7 minutes or until onion starts to brown. Add the broth, beans and dried peppers. Bring to a boil and cook for 15 minutes. Reduce to a simmer.

Remove the peppers and purée them in a small food processor or blender. Add them back to the ingredients in the saucepan. Add the tomato sauce, coffee, sugar, cocoa, oregano, salt, red pepper flakes, coriander, cumin and cayenne. Continue to simmer for 1 hour, stirring occasionally.

Serve hot sprinkled with Cheddar cheese, slices of avocado (if using) or your favourite chili toppings.

DAIRY-FREE OPTION Use dairy-free cheese or make it without.

GLUTEN-FREE OPTION Use gluten-free tempeh.

VEGAN OPTION Use vegan cheese or make it without and replace the brown sugar with organic cane sugar.

> TIP: Why tempeh? This fermented soy product is said to be the closest whole-food soy you can get. Fermented also means it is full of bioactive peptides that make it highly digestible, allowing our bodies to better absorb nutrients. There are studies that recommend tempeh as a significantly concentrated and easily absorbed calcium source that contains a wealth of beneficial plant nutrients.

OYSTER MUSHROOM AND ROSEMARY RAGU ON POLENTA

This sauce of meaty oyster and cremini mushrooms, onion and zucchini will surely win you over! Hearty and satisfyingly complete, we love the ragu topped over pasta, grains or polenta when we want something substantial. Save time by preparing the ragu 1 to 2 days in advance, and simply reheat and add to freshly cooked polenta. Try the Roasted Cauliflower Soup with Tarragon Brown Butter (page 69) as the perfect starter to this meal.

Serves 4 **GF**

OYSTER MUSHROOM AND ROSEMARY RAGU
1 Tbsp (15 mL) grapeseed oil
1 cup (250 mL) diced white or
   yellow onion
1 cup (250 mL) diced zucchini
2 cups (500 mL) chopped
   cremini mushrooms, washed,
   stems trimmed
2 cups (500 mL) chopped king
   oyster mushrooms, washed,
   stems trimmed
½ cup (125 mL) dry red wine
1 cup (250 mL) Simple Vegetable
   Broth (page 62) or low-sodium,
   store-bought vegetable broth
2 Tbsp (30 mL) tomato paste
¼ tsp (1 mL) sea salt
¼ tsp (1 mL) ground black pepper
½ cup (125 mL) 1% milk
2 Tbsp (30 mL) chopped
   fresh rosemary

POLENTA
1½ cups (375 mL) water
½ cup (125 mL) cornmeal
½ cup (125 mL) 1% milk
1 Tbsp (15 mL) unsalted butter
¼ tsp (1 mL) sea salt

Heat a large saucepan over medium heat. Add the oil, onion, zucchini and mushrooms, and sauté until the onion is softened. Add the wine and bring to a boil, stirring often. Reduce to a simmer and add the broth and tomato paste. Continue to simmer for 40 minutes. Season with salt and pepper. Remove from the heat and slowly stir in the milk and rosemary. The ragu should be fairly thick. Set aside and keep warm.

Add the water to a medium saucepan and bring to a boil. Add the cornmeal slowly and stir. Whisk continuously to avoid lumps for 3 to 5 minutes or until thick. Add the milk. Reduce to a simmer and continue to cook for 20 minutes, stirring frequently. Add the butter and salt, and stir. Serve the ragu hot on top of polenta.

> TIP: King oyster mushrooms provide a great base suited for meatless cooking because they're a heavier mushroom and have a thick, meaty flesh that provides wonderful texture.

SCARLET CURRY AND BROILED GARLIC TOFU OVER JASMINE RICE

This is a mild, red coconut curry with baby corn, sweet potato, red pepper and mushrooms. It's jazzed up with the delicious addition of crispy broiled garlic tofu croutons and cilantro, and comes together as a wonderful dinner served over lightly scented Jasmine rice.

Serves 4 to 6   (V)

BROILED GARLIC TOFU
1 package (12 oz/350 g) extra-firm tofu, diced and pressed with a heavy skillet between paper and tea towels for at least 1 hour
1 Tbsp (15 mL) vegetable oil
1½ tsp (7 mL) garlic salt

SCARLET CURRY
2 cups (500 mL) water
1 cup (250 mL) Jasmine rice
1 Tbsp (15 mL) grapeseed oil
½ cup (125 mL) sliced yellow onion
¼ cup (60 mL) Thai red curry paste
1 cup (250 mL) peeled and diced sweet potato
1 package (8 oz/230g) cremini or white button mushrooms, quartered
1 can (14 oz/398 mL) baby corn, halved
1 can (14 oz /398 mL) full-fat coconut milk
1 cup (250 mL) Simple Vegetable Broth (page 62) or low-sodium, store-bought vegetable broth
1 sweet red or green pepper, thinly sliced
¼ cup (60 mL) chopped fresh cilantro or parsley
4 to 6 lime wedges, to garnish (optional)

Place the oven rack in the centre position, and preheat the oven to broil. Line a large baking sheet with parchment paper or a silicone mat and set aside.

Put the tofu cubes in a bowl and gently toss with the vegetable oil. Place cubes evenly on the prepared pan and broil for 3 minutes, flip once and broil for another 3 minutes. Remove them from the oven, place them in the bowl and toss evenly with garlic salt. Set aside.

Place the water and rice in a medium saucepan and bring to a boil. Reduce to a simmer, cover and cook for 10 minutes. Remove from the heat and let sit, covered, for 5 minutes or until ready to use.

Heat a large saucepan on medium-low heat. Add the grapeseed oil and onion, and cook for 5 to 7 minutes or until tender. Stir in the curry paste and heat for an additional few minutes. Add the sweet potato, mushrooms, corn, coconut milk and broth. Simmer, covered, until the sweet potato is tender, about 8 to 10 minutes. Stir in the sweet pepper and simmer an additional 2 minutes. Scoop the rice into serving bowls and top with a ladle or two of the curry. Sprinkle with the crispy tofu pieces and cilantro. Garnish with lime wedges (if using). Serve.

SIGNIFICANT
SALADS

FIVE-MINUTE CUCUMBER AND HERB SALAD

Need a last-minute meal for yourself or guests? Make this stress-free salad! Customize to your taste using fresh mint, dill or both; this salad really is that versatile that it could be served at almost any meal. When seasoned with dill, it would be a delicious accompaniment to Russian, European and Ukrainian dishes or use both mint and dill to serve with Middle Eastern or Indian meals. This recipe is a regular staple at Patricia's house as it is easy to make, even for children. For a complete meal, serve with Miso Vegetable Borscht (page 68) or Orange and Beet Salad with Toasted Walnuts (page 101).

Serves 4 to 6

2 large English cucumbers, cut into slices ¼ inch (5 mm) thick
1 cup (250 mL) plain thick 1% Greek yogurt
1 Tbsp (15 mL) chopped fresh dill or mint (or a combination)
¼ tsp (1 mL) sea salt
Pinch of freshly ground pepper

Place sliced cucumbers in a medium bowl and set aside. Stir together yogurt, herbs, salt and pepper in a small bowl. Add yogurt mixture to cucumber and stir. Make up to 1 hour before serving.

RAW OPTION Replace the Greek yogurt with raw yogurt.

> TIP: 1. Use a wavy chopper or crinkle-cut tool to create a salad that has a bit of a different look to it! Kids love using this tool to make wavy vegetables that are fun to eat. Of course, always supervise children in the kitchen when using this sharp tool. 2. If you are using field cucumbers, peel and remove seeds before making this salad. Use 3 field cucumbers instead of 2 English cucumbers.

TOSSED BABY ARUGULA AND ZUCCHINI SALAD

Lemon and Parmesan cheese are the perfect accents for tender and slightly bitter, baby arugula and crunchy, julienned zucchini strips. Black sea salt is the finishing touch, but if you don't have it, any regular sea salt will do the trick! Try it with the Slow Cooker French Onion Miso Soup (page 76) or the Black Quinoa and Cauliflower Halloumi Cheese Balls (page 44).

Serves 2 **GF**

2 cups (500 mL) baby arugula leaves
2 cups (500 mL) julienned or
   matchstick zucchini strips
½ tsp (2 mL) fresh lemon zest
1 Tbsp (15 mL) fresh lemon juice
1 Tbsp (15 mL) extra virgin olive oil
Pinch of black Himalayan sea salt or
   any sea salt
Pinch of ground black pepper
¼ cup (60 mL) grated Parmesan
   cheese or shaved petals

Rinse and dry the arugula and toss with the zucchini strips in a medium bowl. Add the lemon zest, juice and oil, and toss until well combined. Divide mixture onto 2 plates. Sprinkle each with salt, pepper and 2 Tbsp (30 mL) of Parmesan cheese.

TIP: Not only does black Himalayan sea salt have a unique dark colour, but it also contains plenty of bioavailable minerals and elements that your body can absorb easily, including potassium, iron, sulphur, calcium and magnesium. These trace elements and minerals are what we need for efficient cell metabolism. A little goes a long way . . . you only need a small sprinkle to enjoy the taste of this lovely, smoky salt.

AVOCADO, PINK GRAPEFRUIT AND SAVOY CABBAGE SALAD WITH SUMAC

This fresh and vibrant salad is made with crunchy green savoy cabbage, creamy avocado chunks and invigorating pink grapefruit segments. It's topped with a lightly sweet dressing of apple cider vinegar, maple syrup and extra virgin olive oil scented with tangy, lemony sumac.

Serves 2

2 cups (500 mL) thinly sliced savoy cabbage leaves, chopped into bite-sized pieces
1 cup (250 mL) peeled and chopped pink or Ruby Red grapefruit segments, pith removed
½ cup (125 mL) chopped tomatoes
¼ cup (60 mL) chopped fresh cilantro
1 avocado, peeled, pitted and diced
⅓ cup (75 mL) toasted, chopped cashews
2 Tbsp (30 mL) pure maple syrup
2 Tbsp (30 mL) apple cider vinegar
2 Tbsp (30 mL) extra virgin olive oil
½ tsp (2 mL) ground sumac
Pinch of sea salt

Place the cabbage in a large mixing or salad bowl. Toss with the grapefruit, tomatoes, cilantro, avocado and cashews. Set aside.

Mix the maple syrup, vinegar, oil, sumac and salt in a small bowl. Drizzle the dressing over salad. Serve.

RAW OPTION Replace the toasted cashews with raw cashews and replace the maple syrup with raw agave syrup or raw honey.

> TIP: To toast cashews, preheat the oven to 350°F (180°C) and place the cashews on a baking sheet. Toast for 5 to 7 minutes or until fragrant and golden. Remove from the oven to cool.

CRISP ICEBERG WEDGE SALAD
WITH CASHEWS AND CHILI MANGO DRESSING

The heat of the summer brings a desire for light, refreshing meals. A crisp iceberg lettuce wedge with rice noodles, carrot, bean sprouts, cashews and basil, topped with a tangy dressing fits the bill! Perfect as a meal or side, this salad's dressing can be made up to 3 days in advance. A perfect companion to a yummy glass of Cantaloupe Citrus Gazpacho (page 64).

Serves 4 to 6 **DF** **GF** **V**

CHILI MANGO DRESSING
1 ripe mango, chopped
2 Tbsp (30 mL) sweet chili sauce
2 Tbsp (30 mL) water
Pinch of sea salt

ICEBERG WEDGE SALAD
3 oz (85 g) rice vermicelli noodles
1 head of iceberg lettuce,
   cut into 4 wedges (meal)
   or 6 (side salad)
1 cup (250 mL) bean sprouts
⅓ cup (75 mL) julienned or
   grated carrot
⅓ cup (75 mL) cashew pieces
2 Tbsp (30 mL) chopped fresh basil

TIP: Save and use the lettuce centres for other salads or taco fillings.

Place the mango, chili sauce, water and salt in a blender and purée until smooth. Place in a serving bowl and refrigerate until serving.

Bring 8 cups (2 L) of water to a boil in a medium or large saucepan. Cook the rice noodles until tender, about 5 minutes. Rinse the noodles under cold water, drain and set aside.

Remove the centre of the lettuce from each wedge. Place each wedge on a plate, and fill the inside with about ½ cup (125 mL) of cooked noodles. Top with bean sprouts and carrot. Drizzle the dressing on top and garnish with cashew pieces and fresh basil. Enjoy immediately.

BRAISED RED CHARD AND CURRANT FREEKEH

Freekeh is a green, unripened wheat that has a naturally slightly smoky flavour and tastes delicious alongside pine nuts, tender chard and sweet currants. A nutrition-packed, high-fibre salad with no dressing and only a few simple ingredients makes it suitable for easy dinners and lunches.

Serves 2 **DF** **V**

½ cup (125 mL) freekeh
1 cup (250 mL) water
1 Tbsp (15 mL) grapeseed oil
1 tsp (5 mL) minced garlic
5 cups (1.25 L) red chard, cut into
    1-inch (2.5 cm) strips
½ cup (125 mL) currants
⅓ cup (75 mL) pine nuts
Pinch of sea salt
Pinch of ground black pepper

Place the freekeh and water in a medium saucepan over high heat and bring to a boil. Reduce to a simmer and cover for 20 to 25 minutes until tender. Set aside to cool.

Place the oil and garlic in a skillet or large saucepan over medium-high heat, and sauté for 1 to 2 minutes or until garlic is fragrant. Add the chard and sauté for another 1 to 2 minutes or until the chard is wilted and tender.

In a medium bowl, combine the cooked freekeh, chard, currants and pine nuts, and mix until combined. Season with salt and pepper. Serve.

CRACKED PEPPER COTTAGE CHEESE SALAD
WITH STRAWBERRIES AND TOASTED ALMONDS

Cottage cheese is an excellent low-fat protein source and its creamy taste and texture are complemented by fresh spinach, sweet berries, crunchy almonds and a hit of cracked pepper.

Serves 4 **GF**

¼ cup (60 mL) slivered almonds
4 cups (1 L) lightly packed spinach,
    chiffonade
2 cups (500 mL) creamy
    cottage cheese
1 cup (250 mL) sliced strawberries
¼ cup (60 mL) thinly sliced
    red onion
4 tsp (20 mL) extra virgin olive oil
¼ tsp (1 mL) freshly cracked
    black pepper

Heat a dry saucepan over medium heat. Toast the almonds in the pan until lightly golden and fragrant. Remove from the heat and let cool.

Divide the spinach onto 4 plates. Scoop ½ cup (125 mL) of cottage cheese on the greens, then top with strawberries and sliced onion. Drizzle with a touch of oil. Top with cracked pepper and toasted almonds. Serve immediately.

RAW SHAVED ASPARAGUS SALAD
WITH DULSE AND PARMESAN

Shaved asparagus is served with wonderfully earthy dulse leaves and salty Parmesan petals. A vibrant and easy raw salad for any rushed dinner menu or quick picnic lunch. Add this easy salad to the Roasted Red Pepper and Pumpkin Lasagna (page 188) for a delicious dinner.

Serves 4 **GF**

1 cup (250 mL) dulse leaves
1 bunch asparagus, tough ends trimmed, tips removed and set aside
¼ cup (60 mL) apple cider vinegar
2 Tbsp (30 mL) extra virgin olive oil
2 Tbsp (30 mL) shaved Parmesan cheese petals

Rinse dulse thoroughly so no small shells or stones remain in the leaves. Place in a bowl of water to rehydrate and set aside.

Using a vegetable peeler, remove the outside layer of the asparagus stalk and discard. Shave the remainder of asparagus into thin slices, and place them, along with asparagus tips, onto a large salad plate. Sprinkle asparagus shavings with pieces of rehydrated dulse.

Mix the vinegar and oil and drizzle over top. Sprinkle with Parmesan cheese petals and serve.

> TIP: Create Parmesan cheese petals by using a large cheese slicer or even a vegetable peeler to carve off thin, shaved slices of cheese.

MICROGREEN AND FIG SALAD
WITH HEMP SEED GREMOLATA

A delicious and nourishing salad you can prepare in seconds! A creamy white balsamic and honey dressing is a lively accompaniment to sweet figs, crunchy endive and fresh, living microgreens. When it is topped with a sprinkle of hemp seed gremolata, you are getting a superdose of goodness all in one dish. For a complete dinner, add the Mushroom and Caramelized Onion Pizza with Brie and Maple (page 131).

Serves 4

MICROGREEN AND FIG SALAD

4 cups (1 L) sunflower microgreens or your favourite variety

2 cups (500 mL) sliced endive

4 large figs, trimmed and quartered

DRESSING

¼ cup (60 mL) extra virgin olive oil

2 Tbsp (30 mL) white balsamic vinegar

1 Tbsp (15 mL) liquid honey

2 tsp (10 mL) sour cream or Natural Plain Yogurt (page 195) or plain kefir

Pinch of sea salt

HEMP SEED GREMOLATA

¼ cup (60 mL) finely chopped fresh parsley

⅓ cup (75 mL) raw, shelled hemp seeds

1 tsp (5 mL) fresh lemon zest

1 tsp (5 mL) minced garlic

Sea salt and ground black pepper, to taste

Divide microgreens and sliced endive onto 4 salad plates. Add the quartered figs. Set aside.

Mix the oil, vinegar, honey, sour cream and salt in a glass jar with lid, or whisk in a small bowl. Set aside.

Place the parsley, hemp seeds, lemon zest, garlic, salt and pepper in a small bowl and mix well. Top each microgreen and fig salad with a generous drizzle of dressing and a sprinkle of gremolata.

DAIRY-FREE OPTION Replace the sour cream with coconut, soy or almond milk yogurt or other dairy-free sour cream or yogurt.

VEGAN OPTION Replace the honey with pure maple syrup and the sour cream with coconut, soy or almond milk yogurt or vegan sour cream.

> TIP: How to buy figs? Plump, ripe figs that are slightly wrinkled are the best. Do not buy ones that are shrunken, have any mould or are leaking juice. Also, if the skin is too tight and the fig is too firm, it may not be ripe enough yet.

WATERCRESS, LENTIL AND BEET SALAD WITH POMEGRANATE MOLASSES

Crunchy, peppery watercress is topped with beluga lentils, steamed matchstick beets, crumbles of fresh goat cheese and drizzled pomegranate molasses for a tangy sweet finish. This light, nutrient-packed salad makes a dynamic starter to excite your taste buds or divide this recipe in half for two larger, meal-sized salads.

Serves 4 as a starter or 2 as a main **GF**

½ cup (125 mL) black beluga lentils
1 cup (250 mL) water
4 cups (1 L) raw watercress
2 cups (500 mL) raw golden or red beets, peeled and julienned into matchsticks
½ cup (125 mL) goat cheese
Pomegranate molasses, to taste

Rinse the lentils and place with the water over high heat in a medium saucepan. Bring to a boil, then reduce to a simmer and cover. Continue to cook for 40 to 45 minutes or until the lentils are tender and no water remains in the saucepan. Place the beets in a medium steam saucepan and cook for 5 to 6 minutes or until just tender.

Place 1 cup (250 mL) of watercress on each plate, top with cooked lentils, beets and crumble goat cheese on top. Add a generous drizzle of molasses. Serve.

> TIP: 1. Don't have beluga lentils? Use any of your favourite lentils. You can also replace the goat cheese with a large dollop of plain Greek yogurt. 2. Pomegranate molasses is a sweet, red, berry-like syrup and is usually found in the international food aisle of the grocery store or in Middle Eastern grocery stores.

LEMON AND MINT WILD RICE SALAD WITH FETA AND TOASTED WALNUTS

The texture of chewy wild rice and crunchy walnuts is a perfect foundation for this salad that bursts with a zing of lemon, savoury feta and a touch of fresh mint.

Serves 2 to 4

½ cup (125 mL) wild rice
1½ cups (375 mL) water
1 Tbsp (15 mL) grapeseed oil
¼ cup (60 mL) chopped shallots
½ tsp (2 mL) minced garlic
1 cup (250 mL) Simple Vegetable
   Broth (page 62) or low-sodium,
   store-bought vegetable broth
¼ cup (60 mL) toasted walnuts
1 tsp (5 mL) fresh lemon juice
½ tsp (2 mL) fresh lemon zest
2 Tbsp (30 mL) chopped fresh mint
¼ cup (60 mL) crumbled feta cheese

Soak the wild rice, covered, in water overnight. Rinse the rice and set aside.

Place the oil and shallots in a medium saucepan over medium heat, and sauté until the onion is softened, about 4 to 5 minutes. Add the garlic and wild rice, and sauté for another 1 to 3 minutes to slightly cook garlic.

Add the broth to the saucepan and bring to a boil. Reduce to a simmer and cook, covered, for 50 to 55 minutes or until the rice puffs open and broth is completely absorbed.

Remove from the heat and toss in the walnuts, lemon juice, zest and mint. Add the feta cheese and serve.

ORANGE AND BEET SALAD WITH TOASTED WALNUTS

Colourful citrus and beets are gorgeous together and this salad's flavours will make you love them even more. Tangy oranges and sweet, earthy beets are sprinkled with toasted walnuts, on top of lightly dressed quinoa and fresh parsley. This salad makes a stunning presentation spread across a large serving tray, but it can also be tossed in a large bowl if you prefer. Serve it with the Miso Vegetable Borscht (page 68) or Five-Minute Cucumber and Herb Salad (page 89).

Serves 4

3 small (2-inch/5 cm) golden and/or red beets with skin on
¼ to ⅓ cup (60 to 75 mL) walnuts or pecans
1⅓ cups (325 mL) water
⅔ cup (150 mL) quinoa
2 Tbsp (30 mL) grapeseed oil
2 Tbsp (30 mL) red wine vinegar
2 Tbsp (30 mL) chopped fresh parsley
Pinch of ground chipotle pepper
½ tsp (2 mL) liquid honey
¼ tsp (1 mL) sea salt
Pinch of ground black pepper
1 orange, rind removed, cut into slices ¼ inch (5 mm) thick
1 pink grapefruit, rind removed, cut into slices ¼ inch (5 mm) thick
3 Tbsp (45 mL) thinly sliced green onion
Microgreens, to garnish (optional)

In a small saucepan, cover the beets with water and bring to a boil. Cook until tender, about 12 minutes. Pour off the water and place the beets in ice water. When cool, peel the beet skins and cut the flesh into slices ¼ inch (5 mm) thick. Set aside.

Preheat the oven to 350°F (180°C). Place the walnuts on a baking sheet. Bake for 5 to 7 minutes or until toasted and fragrant. Remove from the oven and let cool. Coarsely chop and set aside.

Bring the water and quinoa to a boil in a medium saucepan. Reduce to a simmer. Cover and cook for 10 minutes. Turn off the heat and let sit, covered, for an additional 5 minutes. Remove the lid to cool completely.

Whisk the oil, vinegar, parsley, chipotle pepper, honey, salt and pepper in a medium bowl. Stir in the cooled quinoa and spread across a large serving tray. Place the beets, orange, grapefruit, walnuts and green onion over the quinoa. Garnish with microgreens (if using). Serve.

VEGAN OPTION Replace the honey with pure maple syrup.

> TIP: As an alternative, you can replace the cooked quinoa with 2 cups (500 mL) of any other favourite cooked ancient grain. As well, when in season, blood oranges are a beautiful addition to this salad.

LAZY LAYERED SALAD
WITH HERBED KEFIR RANCH DRESSING

Typically meant to feed a large crowd, layered salads are always a favourite because of their colourful, fresh display. This salad easily feeds a smaller group or you may want to double or triple the ingredients to make a larger serving when entertaining guests. The rich and tangy dressing is addictive, so be careful not to leave this dish alone for too long; it'll be eaten up quickly! Cheesy Veggie Joes (page 139) make a great addition, as well as the Hot Barbecue Veggie and Superslaw Sandwiches (page 137) or even the Cheesy Cauliflower and Sweet Potato Bake (page 157).

Serves 4 to 8

HERBED KEFIR RANCH DRESSING

½ cup (125 mL) plain kefir
⅓ cup (75 mL) 14% sour cream
¼ cup (60 mL) Creamy Mayonnaise (page 197) or store-bought
1 Tbsp (15 mL) thinly sliced fresh chives
2 tsp (10 mL) fresh basil leaves, chiffonade
¼ tsp (1 mL) dry mustard
1 tsp (5 mL) pure maple syrup
¼ tsp (1 mL) fine sea salt, or to taste
Pinch of freshly ground pepper

LAZY LAYERED SALAD

1½ heads of Romaine lettuce, outer leaves removed
1½ cups (375 mL) sliced Roma tomatoes
1 sweet yellow pepper, diced
1 cup (250 mL) sliced purple cauliflower
¾ cup (175 mL) shredded Cheddar cheese
Microgreens, to garnish (optional)

Whisk the kefir, sour cream, mayonnaise, chives, basil, mustard, maple syrup, salt and pepper together in vessel you can pour from. Cover and refrigerate until serving.

Pile the romaine leaves at one end of a large platter. Add a layer of tomatoes beside them. Next add a layer of the yellow pepper and then purple cauliflower. Place the Cheddar cheese in a line beside the cauliflower. Garnish with microgreens (if using). Serve the salad with the dressing on the side to pour. The dressing will last for up to 3 days in the refrigerator.

DAIRY-FREE OPTION Replace the kefir with almond or coconut kefir, the sour cream with cashew sour cream and the Cheddar cheese with soy, nut or seed cheese or other dairy-free cheese.

VEGAN OPTION Replace the kefir with almond or coconut kefir, the sour cream with cashew sour cream, the mayonnaise with vegan mayonnaise and the Cheddar cheese with soy, nut or seed cheese or other vegan cheese.

> TIP: 1. A chiffonade is slicing leaves into long ribbons by first stacking them flat together, then tightly rolling and slicing them. 2. Make this salad a meal by adding toasted walnuts, pecans or almonds and a sliced boiled egg.

SUPERSLAW

Coleslaw is a timeless go-to side dish in many countries around the world. Our take on classic coleslaw is upgraded with pepitas, a twist of fresh lime and cilantro. Its popularity is due to its versatility and stable refrigerator-life. A vinegar-based dressing makes it lower in calories too. This slaw can be made up to 3 days in advance. It's great served with the Jamaican Jerk Tofu (page 149) and the Caribbean Coconut and Black Bean Quinoa (page 57).

Serves 4 to 6

¼ cup (60 mL) raw pepitas
1¾ cups (425 mL) thinly sliced
　green cabbage
½ cup (125 mL) thinly sliced
　purple cabbage
1 cup (250 mL) grated carrot
4 green onions, thinly sliced
2 Tbsp (30 mL) walnut oil, grape-
　seed oil or light flavoured oil
2 Tbsp (30 mL) apple cider vinegar
2 Tbsp (30 mL) chopped
　fresh cilantro
1 Tbsp (15 mL) liquid honey
2 tsp (10 mL) minced pickled
　jalapeño peppers (optional)
Squeeze of fresh lime juice
½ tsp (2 mL) sea salt

Heat a dry saucepan or skillet over medium heat. Place the pepitas in the pan and stir every 20 seconds until toasted and fragrant (5 to 6 minutes). Remove the pan from the heat and place the pepitas in a medium bowl to cool.

Place both cabbages, the carrot and green onions in a bowl. Whisk together the oil, vinegar, cilantro, honey, jalapeños (if using), lime juice and salt. Pour over the vegetable mixture, toss, sprinkle with the reserved pepitas and serve.

VEGAN OPTION Replace the honey with pure maple syrup.

RAW OPTION Do not toast the raw pepitas and make sure to use raw honey.

> TIP: When buying apple cider vinegar, opt for unfiltered and organic. This ensures a perfectly pure flavour filled with valuable health properties.

FARRO AND KALE SALAD
WITH BASIL, ORANGE AND CRANBERRIES

We love the fantastic crunch and texture of farro and smoky pine nuts with fresh chopped kale and the lively flavour of lemon and basil pesto. This is a great option for a side salad or a filling and tasty lunch entrée. We also recommend serving it alongside the Steel-Cut Oat Shepherd's Pie with Parsnip, Cauliflower and Potato Mash with Sage (page 165).

Serves 2 to 4 **DF**

½ cup (125 mL) farro
1 cup (250 mL) water
2½ tsp (12 mL) basil pesto (see Tip)
1½ tsp (7 mL) liquid honey
1 Tbsp (15 mL) fresh orange juice
2 tsp (10 mL) fresh orange zest
1 Tbsp (15 mL) orange blossom
     water (optional)
Pinch of sea salt (optional)
¾ cup (175 mL) chopped kale
¼ cup (60 mL) pine nuts
¼ cup (60 mL) chopped dried
     cranberries

Place the farro and water in a medium saucepan and bring to a boil. Reduce to a simmer and cook, covered, for 25 to 30 minutes or until the farro is fluffy and no water remains in the saucepan.

Whisk the pesto, honey, orange juice, zest, orange blossom water (if using) and salt (if using) in a small bowl, and pour into the saucepan over the cooked farro. Toss in the kale, pine nuts and cranberries. Stir to combine. Serve.

VEGAN OPTION Replace the honey with pure maple syrup.

TIP: 1. Your new favourite secret ingredient? Often used in Lebanese cooking, orange blossom water can add a lovely floral aroma to savoury and sweet cooked grains and salads and many other dishes. It can also be used in the bath, in body lotions or as a facial toner. It can often be found in Asian grocery stores or specialty cooking stores. 2. Making your own basil pesto is easy! Blend 4 cups (1 L) fresh basil leaves, ¼ cup (60 mL) pine nuts, ⅓ cup (75 mL) extra virgin olive oil, 2 cloves garlic and ¼ cup (60 mL) Parmesan cheese in a food processor or blender. Season with a touch of salt and voila!

CREAMY CURRY, CHICKPEA, BROCCOLI AND RED PEPPER SALAD

Slightly sweetened curry dressing lightly blankets the chickpeas, red pepper and broccoli in this healthy salad. One of our favourites, broccoli is known to be a cancer-fighting superhero, not to mention a nutritional powerhouse, with 9 grams of fibre and a slim 44 calories per 1 cup (250 mL). Bulk up the salad to make a meal by serving it with the Caribbean Coconut and Black Bean Quinoa (page 57) or Coconut Chili Lime Collard Green Wraps (page 123).

Serves 4 to 6 **GF**

2 cups (500 mL) cooked chickpeas or 1 can (19 oz/540 mL) chickpeas, drained and rinsed
2 cups (500 mL) broccoli chopped into 1-inch (2.5 cm) pieces
1 red pepper, diced
½ cup (125 mL) Creamy Mayonnaise (page 197) or store-bought
½ cup (125 mL) plain thick 1% Greek yogurt
2 tsp (10 mL) extra virgin olive oil
1 tsp (5 mL) liquid honey
½ tsp (2 mL) Dijon mustard
½ tsp (2 mL) fresh lemon juice
¼ tsp and a pinch (1.5 mL) curry powder
¼ tsp (1 mL) sea salt
Pinch of freshly ground pepper

Place the chickpeas, broccoli and red pepper in a medium bowl.

Whisk together the mayonnaise, yogurt, oil, honey, Dijon, lemon juice, curry powder, salt and pepper. Stir the dressing into the vegetable mixture. Serve.

DAIRY-FREE OPTION Replace the yogurt with coconut, soy or almond milk yogurt or other dairy-free yogurt.

VEGAN OPTION Replace the mayonnaise with vegan mayonnaise, the yogurt with coconut, soy or almond milk yogurt and the honey with pure maple syrup.

TIP: You can add the dressing up to 3 hours before serving.

CHARRED CORN AND ROASTED VEGETABLE SUMMER SALAD WITH PEACHES AND LIME HERBED BUTTERMILK DRESSING

Sweet corn, gently charred for that rich, smoky flavour is tossed with a colourful medley of hearty roasted vegetables, then accented with a blast of fresh veggies and summer peaches to deliver a complete spectrum of taste and satisfaction along with a zesty citrus, herbed buttermilk dressing. This striking dish is sure to impress at your social gatherings all summer long and makes a tasty partner to the Guacamole Portobello Burgers with Miso Barbecue Sauce (page 138).

Serves 8 to 10

CHARRED CORN AND ROASTED VEGETABLE SALAD

2 cups (500 mL) large diced
    zucchini, skin on
2 cups (500 mL) large diced
    eggplant
2 large peaches, pitted,
    sliced into wedges
½ cup (125 mL) chopped Vidalia
    or yellow onion
2 cups (500 mL) charred corn
    kernels (see Tip)
1 cup (250 mL) shelled
    fresh edamame
1 cup (250 mL) halved grape
    tomatoes
2 avocados, peeled, pitted and diced

LIME HERBED BUTTERMILK DRESSING

½ cup (125 mL) Natural Plain Yogurt
    (page 195) or store-bought
¼ cup (60 mL) buttermilk
½ cup (125 mL) finely chopped
    fresh cilantro
2 Tbsp (30 mL) pure maple syrup
1 tsp (5 mL) minced garlic
1 Tbsp (15 mL) fresh lime juice
1 tsp (5 mL) fresh lime zest
¼ tsp (1 mL) smoked paprika
Pinch of sea salt

Preheat the oven to 450°F (230°C) and line a large baking sheet with parchment paper. Place the zucchini, eggplant, peaches and onion on the prepared baking sheet, and roast for 10 to 14 minutes, tossing occasionally to ensure the vegetables are evenly roasted. Remove from the oven and let cool slightly.

For the dressing, place the yogurt, buttermilk, cilantro, maple syrup, garlic, lime juice, zest, paprika and salt in a medium bowl and mix well. Set aside.

Place the corn, edamame and tomatoes in a large bowl, and add the roasted vegetables. Add the avocado and toss gently. Add the dressing and toss until the salad is well combined. Serve slightly cooled.

> TIP: Char corn cobs on the barbecue, an indoor grill, a skillet or a roasting pan in the oven. Grill or sear peeled cobs on high heat until the kernels have dark toasted spots. After the cobs have cooled slightly, hold the cob vertically and slice off the kernels. Or roast the cobs on a baking sheet in the oven at 500°F (300°C), turning often, or in a skillet on high until char marks appear. If all you have is a bag of frozen corn, char in a skillet on the stovetop.

LENTIL CAKE SALAD
WITH ROASTED RED PEPPER AND FETA

This is a great salad-for-dinner option! Lentils are often a favourite meat substitute because they're a great source of lean protein and have plenty of dietary fibre. If you don't require gluten-free, any rolled oats will do!

Serves 4 to 6

LENTIL CAKES
½ cup (125 mL) walnut or
   pecan pieces
1¾ cups (425 mL) Simple Vegetable
   Broth (page 62) or low-sodium,
   store-bought vegetable broth
¾ cup (175 mL) French green lentils,
   sorted and rinsed
½ cup (125 mL) chopped onion
¾ cup (175 mL) gluten-free
   rolled oats
1 Tbsp (15 mL) fresh lemon juice
¾ tsp (3 mL) sea salt
1 to 2 tsp (5 to 10 mL) minced garlic
1 tsp (5 mL) ground cumin
¼ tsp (1 mL) cracked black pepper

DRESSING
¼ cup (60 mL) unrefined
   cold-pressed walnut oil
   or vegetable oil
1 Tbsp (15 mL) minced shallots
1½ Tbsp (22 mL) white
   wine vinegar
1 tsp (5 mL) mild Dijon mustard
1 tsp (5 mL) liquid honey

SALAD
1 package (5 oz/140 g) mixed greens
1 roasted red pepper, skin and
   seeds removed and thinly sliced
¼ cup (60 mL) crumbled feta cheese

Toast the walnuts in a dry medium saucepan over medium heat for 5 to 6 minutes or until fragrant and toasted. Remove from the heat and let cool.

Place the broth, lentils and onion in a medium saucepan. Bring to a boil over medium-high heat. Reduce to a simmer, cover and cook for 30 minutes. Remove from the heat and let sit, covered, for an additional 10 minutes. Remove the lid and allow to cool.

Preheat the oven to 375°F (190°C). Line a large baking sheet with parchment paper and set aside.

Place the lentil mixture, toasted walnuts, oats, lemon juice, salt, garlic, cumin and pepper in a food processor with an S blade. Pulse until the walnuts and lentils are in about ¼-inch (5 mm) pieces and you can press the mixture into a patty. Form the mixture into patties that are 2 inches (5 cm) wide and about ½ inch (1 cm) thick, and place on the prepared baking sheet. Bake for 8 to 9 minutes until golden brown on each side.

Whisk together the oil, shallots, vinegar, Dijon and honey in a small bowl. Toss with the mixed greens. Plate the greens and top with the roasted red pepper, feta cheese and lentil cakes. Serve.

VEGAN OPTION Replace the honey with pure maple syrup and the feta cheese with vegan feta cheese.

> TIP: Don't want to pay high prices for a jar of roasted red peppers? Make them yourself! See page 199.

WARM CAULIFLOWER AND CHICKPEA MIXED GREEN SALAD WITH WHITE BALSAMIC VINAIGRETTE

Satisfy serious hunger with this roasted and seasoned cauliflower and chickpea salad. Chickpeas— also known as garbanzo beans—are roasted and take on a different personality. They're transformed into golden, savoury and very addictive, crunchy little morsels in this warm salad full of dietary fibre and protein. For a bigger meal, serve with the Rustic Farmhouse Soup (page 78).

Serves 4 to 6   **DF GF V**

ROASTED CHICKPEAS

1 can (19 oz/540 mL) chickpeas, drained and rinsed
1 Tbsp (15 mL) grapeseed oil or vegetable oil
½ tsp (2 mL) garlic powder
¼ tsp (1 mL) sea salt
Pinch of ground black pepper
Pinch of ground bay leaf

ROASTED CAULIFLOWER

1 small head of cauliflower, cut into bite-sized pieces
2 Tbsp (30 mL) grapeseed oil or vegetable oil
¼ tsp (1 mL) sea salt
Pinch of ground black pepper

WHITE BALSAMIC VINAIGRETTE

⅓ cup (75 mL) grapeseed oil
3 Tbsp (45 mL) white balsamic vinegar
¼ tsp (1 mL) sea salt
Pinch of dry mustard

SALAD

1 package (5 oz/140 g) mixed greens, such as baby romaine, oak leaf lettuce, Swiss chard, arugula, spinach, frisée and radicchio
¼ cup (60 mL) sliced red onion

Preheat the oven to 425°F (220°C). Line two baking sheets with parchment paper and set aside.

Place the rinsed chickpeas on a clean kitchen towel and dry them. Toss them with the oil in a medium bowl, then place them on one parchment-lined baking sheet. Sprinkle with garlic powder, salt, black pepper and ground bay leaf.

Toss the cauliflower with the oil in the medium bowl and place on the second baking sheet. Sprinkle with salt and pepper. Place both pans in the oven, one on the upper and one on the lower oven rack, and bake for 10 minutes. Reverse the positions of the pans, stir and bake for an additional 10 minutes.

Whisk the oil, vinegar, salt and mustard together in a small bowl. Just before serving, toss the greens with the vinaigrette. Place the greens and red onion onto plates. Add the roasted cauliflower and chickpeas, and serve. Save any extra roasted chickpeas for a great snack.

KOREAN BARBECUE SALAD

Warm salads are incredibly satisfying, especially this one! Korean barbecue skewers of marinated tofu, green pepper and onion are served with fresh mandarin segments, quinoa and romaine lettuce, drizzled with a hot, sweet and salty dressing.

Serves 4 to 6 **DF**

MARINATED TOFU

⅓ cup (75 mL) soy sauce
½ cup (125 mL) liquid honey
1 Tbsp (15 mL) minced garlic
2 Tbsp (30 mL) toasted sesame oil
¼ tsp (1 mL) dried red chili flakes
1 package (12 oz/350 g) extra-firm
   tofu, pressed with a heavy skillet
   between paper towels for at least
   1 hour, cut into 24 cubes

1 cup (250 mL) water
½ cup (125 mL) quinoa
1 green pepper, cut into 1-inch
   (2.5 cm) square pieces
⅔ cup (150 mL) red onion, diced
   into 1-inch (2.5 cm) cubes
2 scallions, cut into 2-inch (5 cm)
   lengths
6 cups (1.5 L) romaine lettuce
   chopped into bite-sized pieces
2 fresh Mandarin oranges, segments
   peeled, skin and pith removed or
   1 can (10 oz/284 mL) Mandarin
   orange segments, juice reserved
   for another recipe
Black sesame seeds, to garnish

Soak 12 standard 10-inch (25 cm) bamboo skewers in water for at least 30 minutes, to ensure they will not burn on the barbecue.

Whisk the soy sauce, honey, garlic, oil and red chili flakes in a small bowl. Place the tofu cubes in a large resealable plastic bag or a medium bowl. Pour the marinade over the tofu cubes and toss to coat. Marinate in the refrigerator for 1 hour or overnight. Stir or turn halfway through marinating.

Bring the water and quinoa to a boil in a medium saucepan. Cover and reduce to a simmer. Simmer for 10 minutes. Turn the heat off but leave covered and set aside for an additional 5 minutes, then fluff with a fork and set aside again.

Preheat the barbecue to 400°F (200°C). Drain the water from the skewers. Alternate skewering the tofu cubes, green pepper, red onion and scallions, leaving 1 inch (2.5 cm) bare on each end of the skewers. Place the reserved marinade in a small saucepan. Bring to a simmer on low heat. Cook until hot. Set aside.

Oil the hot grill with a clean cloth. Place the skewers on the grill about 1 to 2 inches (2.5 to 5 cm) apart. Cook for 5 minutes on one side until the tofu has browned and caramelized. Flip the skewers and cook for another 5 minutes until the vegetables are tender-crisp.

Divide the romaine among plates, then add the quinoa to each. Top with tofu skewers, mandarin segments and black sesame seeds. Drizzle with hot marinade. Serve immediately.

GLUTEN-FREE OPTION Replace the soy sauce with gluten-free tamari.

VEGAN OPTION Replace the honey with pure maple syrup.

WRAPS, BURGERS, SANDWICHES AND PIZZA

WHOLE WHEAT SOFT FLOUR TORTILLAS

Soft and tender, these easy-to-use tortillas are perfect for your favourite quesadillas, burritos, enchiladas, wraps or sandwiches! It's hard to find a store-bought soft tortilla that doesn't contain high levels of sodium, but making your own means you can avoid all the added preservatives and feel good about serving them to your family and friends.

Makes 16 medium (8-inch/20 cm) tortillas, serves 16 DF V

3½ cups (875 mL) whole wheat flour
1½ tsp (7 mL) sea salt
1 tsp (5 mL) baking powder
2 Tbsp (30 mL) grapeseed oil
1½ cups (375 mL) boiling water

OPTIONS

Sandwich wraps or pinwheel slices: Spread with cream cheese, a dash of basil pesto and baby spinach and enjoy as a wrap or sliced as a delightful appetizer.

Crisp crackers: Brush with grapeseed oil and sea salt, gently score with cookie cutters or a pizza wheel and bake for 4 to 5 minutes at 400°F (200°C). Allow to cool and break apart into crackers. Serve with your favourite dips or spreads.

Personal pizzas: Add sauce, oils or pesto and your favourite pizza toppings. Bake for 4 to 5 minutes at 400°F (200°C) until the cheese is melted and the edges are crispy.

Whisk flour, salt and baking powder in a large bowl or stand mixer with whisk attachment. Switch to the dough hook and slowly add the oil and water. Mix until the dough forms a ball, scraping the sides of the bowl as necessary. Divide dough into halves and keep dividing until you have 16 equal-sized pieces of dough. Roll each into a ball approximately 1½ to 2 inches (4 to 5 cm) in diameter. Flatten each ball and allow to rest under a lightly moistened kitchen towel on the counter for 20 minutes.

Heat a large skillet to medium-high. On a well-floured surface, roll each dough ball into a circle about 7 to 8 inches (17.5 to 20 cm) in diameter. Use additional flour as required to prevent the dough from sticking. Place a rolled tortilla into the preheated skillet and cook for 1 to 2 minutes on the first side, until small brown spots appear. Then flip and cook for 30 seconds to 1 minute on the other side until brown spots appear again.

Let cool and store in a resealable plastic bag or container for up to 5 days. Gently reheat in a skillet or in a microwave oven. Freeze for up to 1 month in resealable bags or containers with the tortillas separated by waxed paper or parchment paper.

> TIP: If you want even prettier wraps, try using 2 cups (500 mL) of regular all-purpose flour and 1½ cups (175 mL) of blue corn flour. The result is a lovely pale blue tortilla!

ZUCCHINI WRAPS

It only takes 4 ingredients to make this simple recipe. Baked, these flat wraps are pliable and sturdy so you can use them layered or rolled up. A light, neutral flavour makes them a great base for any of your favourite sandwich or burrito fillings, and they are a tasty partner to the Chipotle Refried Beans (page 55).

Makes 8 small (6-inch/15 cm) wraps

2 to 3 medium-sized zucchini,
    cut into chunks
2 large eggs, lightly beaten
⅓ cup (75 mL) psyllium husk
¼ tsp (1 mL) sea salt

> TIP: Short on time? You can prep your zucchini the same day, but you'll have to spend more time wringing out the zucchini in the cheesecloth.

Purée zucchini in a food processor or high-speed blender, ensuring you have 2 cups (500 mL) or slightly more purée. Place in a paper-towel-lined strainer (or clean kitchen towel or cheesecloth) and chill overnight in the refrigerator. The next day, discard any liquid and place the purée in a cheesecloth or clean kitchen towel and wring out any remaining liquid. Ensure you still have 2 cups (500 mL) of zucchini purée.

Preheat the oven to 350°F (180°C). Line two large baking sheets with parchment paper and set aside. Mix the zucchini and eggs in a large bowl. Add the psyllium husk and salt and mix well into a sticky dough.

Using a ⅓ cup (75 mL) measuring cup or scoop, scoop out the mixture and form into balls. Place them 5 inches (12.5 cm) apart on prepared baking sheets. Place a glass of water at your workspace and, using slightly damp fingers, gently press out each tortilla until it becomes a flat circle, about 6 inches (15 cm) in diameter.

Bake for 5 to 6 minutes until golden brown. Gently peel away from the parchment paper and flip the tortillas to the other side. Return to the oven for another 5 to 6 minutes. Remove from the oven and allow to cool slightly before serving, or chill and serve cold. Store in the refrigerator for up to 5 days.

RIPE PEACH AND PISTACHIO BUTTER LETTUCE WRAPS

Enjoy these wraps as a fresh and light summer lunch or appetizer. We love the contrast of the ripe peaches, sprinkled with toasted pistachios and creamy crumbled blue cheese. Salty, sweet and tangy is a winning combination!

Serves 4 to 8

⅓ cup (75 mL) raw pistachios
1½ Tbsp (22 mL) minced red onion
1½ Tbsp (22 mL) white
    balsamic vinegar
1½ Tbsp (22 mL) grapeseed oil
    or light-tasting oil
Pinch of sea salt
2 ripe peaches, pitted and diced
1 head butter lettuce, leaves
    separated and trimmed if
    too large (12 leaves)
⅓ cup (75 mL) crumbled
    blue cheese

Heat a dry sauté pan over medium heat. Place the pistachios in the pan, stirring frequently, until toasted and fragrant. Remove from the heat and let cool. Set aside.

Whisk together the onion, vinegar, oil and salt in a small bowl. Toss the peach pieces with the dressing until completely coated.

Place the lettuce leaves on plates or a serving tray. Spoon the peach mixture in a line along the rib of the leaf. Repeat with the remaining leaves. Sprinkle each with the toasted pistachios and the crumbled blue cheese. Fold and enjoy.

ROASTED TOMATO, GARLIC, ARUGULA AND GOAT CHEESE FLATBREAD

This flavour-packed flatbread with roasted tomatoes and garlic is topped with fresh arugula and creamy, smooth goat cheese. It makes a great addition to a tapas spread, as a side dish or even as a meal for two. We love serving it with the Mighty Mediterranean Minestrone (page 75) or the Miso Vegetable Borscht (page 68).

Serves 4 as a side or 2 as a main

FLATBREAD CRUST
1 cup (250 mL) whole wheat flour
1 cup (250 mL) all-purpose flour
1 tsp (5 mL) baking powder
¼ tsp (1 mL) sea salt
2 tsp (10 mL) fresh thyme
2 Tbsp (30 mL) grapeseed oil
1 large egg, beaten
⅔ cup (150 mL) water

ROASTED TOMATO, GARLIC, ARUGULA AND GOAT CHEESE TOPPING
2 large tomatoes, diced
2 tsp (10 mL) minced garlic
1 Tbsp (15 mL) balsamic vinegar
1 Tbsp (15 mL) olive oil or
   grapeseed oil
1 Tbsp (15 mL) fresh thyme
½ tsp (2 mL) organic cane sugar
   or white sugar
½ tsp (2 mL) fresh lemon juice
Pinch of sea salt
½ cup (125 mL) goat cheese
¾ cup (175 mL) arugula

Preheat the oven to 425°F (220°C). Line a 13- × 9-inch (3.5 L) baking pan with parchment paper and set aside.

For the crust, place the flours, baking powder, salt, thyme, grapeseed oil, egg and water in a medium bowl, and mix the dough until a ball forms. Spread the dough evenly to reach all sides of prepared pan. Set aside.

Toss the tomatoes, garlic, vinegar, olive oil, thyme, sugar, lemon juice and salt in a medium bowl. Spread the tomato mixture evenly over the flatbread dough. Top evenly with goat cheese crumbles.

Place in the oven and bake for 15 to 20 minutes or until the edges of the crust are crispy and brown. Remove from the oven and top with the fresh arugula. Slice and serve hot.

GLUTEN-FREE OPTION Replace the crust with Zucchini Wraps (page 118), Cauliflower Pizza Crust (page 128) or any gluten-free pizza crust.

COCONUT CHILI LIME
COLLARD GREEN WRAPS

Fresh, raw collard green leaves make strong, hearty wraps, yet they are a tender and delicious alternative to flour-based tortillas. Their mild flavour is a perfect match for these spicy coconut lentils. Topped with tomatoes and shredded aged Cheddar cheese, this is a colourful, handheld meal that will soon become a favourite. If you're hungry for a side salad, add the Lazy Layered Salad (page 102).

Serves 2

4 large collard green leaves
1 cup (250 mL) light coconut milk
½ cup (125 mL) red lentils
1 tsp (5 mL) minced garlic
1 Tbsp (15 mL) pure maple syrup
1 Tbsp (15 mL) Sriracha hot sauce
2 Tbsp (30 mL) fresh lime juice
1 tsp (5 mL) fresh lime zest
1 tsp (5 mL) soy sauce
¼ cup (60 mL) diced tomatoes
¼ cup (60 mL) chopped
   fresh cilantro
2 Tbsp (30 mL) shredded aged
   Cheddar cheese

Wash and dry the collard green leaves and set aside.

Combine the coconut milk and lentils in a medium saucepan. Cover and bring to a boil, then reduce the heat and simmer for about 15 to 20 minutes or until the lentils are soft and the mixture is thick. Stir the mixture often to ensure it does not stick to the saucepan. Add the garlic, maple syrup, hot sauce, lime juice, zest and soy sauce to the lentil mixture.

Place 3 to 4 Tbsp (45 to 60 mL) of lentil mixture in the centre of each collard green leaf, top with tomatoes and sprinkle with cilantro and Cheddar cheese. Serve hot.

DAIRY-FREE OPTION Replace the Cheddar cheese with soy, nut or seed cheese or other dairy-free cheese.

GLUTEN-FREE OPTION Replace the soy sauce with gluten-free tamari.

VEGAN OPTION Replace the Cheddar cheese with soy, nut or seed cheese or other vegan cheese.

> TIP: When buying collard greens, look for large, fresh and rubbery deep-green leaves with no wilting or blemishes.

CHIPOTLE SWEET POTATO TACOS WITH GRILLED PINEAPPLE SALSA

These sweet and zesty tacos please all taste buds and are a perfectly easy, warm-weather dinner. Smoky, grilled sweet potato is tossed with chili pepper and slightly sweetened with tangy pineapple salsa and wrapped in a warm corn tortilla. Sweet potato is a great meatless alternative and the foundation in this dish because of its weight, texture and ability to hold its own as a filling. The Maple and Sumac Baked Beans (page 148) are a delicious side you can serve with this dish.

Serves 4 DF GF V

GRILLED PINEAPPLE SALSA

1 can (14 oz/398 mL) pineapple
  slices, juice drained
2 Roma tomatoes, diced
3 Tbsp (45 mL) minced red onion
2 Tbsp (30 mL) chopped
  fresh cilantro
½ tsp (2 mL) minced garlic
1 Tbsp (15 mL) fresh lime juice
¼ tsp (1 mL) sea salt

CHIPOTLE SWEET POTATO TACOS

2 lb (900 g) sweet potato, cut into
  ¾-inch (2 cm) wide sticks (about
  32 sticks)
1 Tbsp (15 mL) grapeseed oil or
  vegetable oil
¼ tsp (1 mL) ground chipotle
  pepper
¼ tsp (1 mL) sea salt
8 small (6-inch/15 cm) corn tortillas
¼ cup (60 mL) sour cream (optional)
4 lime wedges, to garnish (optional)

Preheat the barbecue to medium temperature and place the pineapple on the grill. Turn the pineapple when lightly grilled, about 5 minutes each side. Let the pineapple cool slightly and dice. In a medium bowl, toss the pineapple with the tomatoes, onion, cilantro, garlic, lime juice and salt. Set aside at room temperature to allow the flavours to mix.

Gently toss the sweet potato pieces with the oil, chipotle pepper and salt. Brush the grill with oil if necessary. Place the sweet potato sticks on the grill. Flip after 7 minutes or so. The sweet potato may become slightly blackened, but don't worry; this will add flavour. Cook for another 7 minutes or until tender. Set aside.

Heat a dry skillet. Warm each tortilla and place in a covered dish. Place 4 sweet potato sticks in each tortilla and top with approximately 2 Tbsp (30 mL) of salsa and 1 Tbsp (15 mL) of sour cream (if using). Garnish with lime wedges (if using). Enjoy immediately.

PORTOBELLO AND PEPPER FAJITAS

Large, meaty-thick mushroom slices are marinated and grilled with your choice of sweet peppers and onions, served in a warm tortilla along with avocado, cheese, salsa and whatever other fajita fixings you crave! For even more flavour, prepare extra marinade seasoning (without the water) and sprinkle on top of the grilling vegetables.

Serves 4

MARINADE
1 cup (250 mL) water
1 tsp (5 mL) cracked black pepper
1 tsp (5 mL) onion powder
1 tsp (5 mL) paprika
1 tsp (5 mL) dried thyme
½ tsp (2 mL) garlic powder
½ tsp (2 mL) ground cumin
½ tsp (2 mL) cayenne pepper

FAJITAS
1 to 2 Tbsp (15 to 30 mL)
    grapeseed oil
6 to 8 large (12 oz/350 g)
    portobello mushroom caps,
    stems trimmed and caps sliced
    into ¾-inch (2 cm) strips
2 cups (500 mL) sliced sweet red,
    yellow or green pepper
1 cup (250 mL) sliced white or
    yellow onion
12 medium (8-inch/20 cm) Whole
    Wheat Soft Flour Tortillas
    (page 117) or store-bought whole
    wheat flour tortillas
Optional toppings when serving:
    shredded aged Cheddar cheese,
    slices of avocado, spicy salsa,
    guacamole, Natural Plain Yogurt
    (page 195) or sour cream

Combine the water, black pepper, onion powder, paprika, thyme, garlic powder, cumin and cayenne pepper and set aside. Place the mushrooms in a shallow dish and pour the marinade over top. Place in refrigerator and allow to marinate for 1 to 2 hours or overnight.

Heat a large sauté pan on medium heat and add the oil. Place the mushroom slices cut side down in the hot pan. Add the red pepper and onion to the pan, and grill until the mushrooms are browned and dark around the edges, the red pepper is softened with some charring on the edges and the onion is golden brown. Reduce the heat to low and place the soft flour tortillas on top of grilling vegetables to warm for 3 to 4 minutes.

Remove the tortillas and vegetables from the pan, placing each in separate serving dishes so that each person can build their own fajitas. To build a fajita, place grilled mushroom, red pepper and onion strips on the tortillas first, then add your favourite optional toppings. Serve.

GLUTEN-FREE OPTION Replace the Whole Wheat Soft Flour Tortillas with gluten-free tortillas.

QUINOA, BEAN AND CHEESE FREEZER BURRITOS

These delicious vegetarian burritos have the nutritional boost of ancient grains, while still retaining an authentic taste with refried beans, cheese and aromatic spices typical of Mexican cuisine. The burritos are stored in the freezer, ready to heat-and-eat in a snap—a quick supper or lunch the kids can easily prepare on their own. If you require this recipe to be dairy-free or vegan, you can easily replace the Cheddar cheese with soy, nut or seed cheese, or other dairy-free or vegan cheese.

Makes 8 burritos

1½ cups (375 mL) water
½ cup (125 mL) quinoa
1 Tbsp (15 mL) smoked paprika
1½ tsp (7 mL) ground cumin
2½ tsp (12 mL) chili powder
2 tsp (10 mL) ground coriander
½ tsp (2 mL) black pepper
½ tsp (2 mL) onion powder
½ tsp (2 mL) garlic powder
½ tsp (2 mL) dried oregano
2 Tbsp (30 mL) grapeseed oil
1½ cups (375 mL) diced
   yellow onion
1 can (27 oz/765 mL) refried beans
   or 3 cups (750 mL) Chipotle
   Refried Beans (page 55)
1½ cups (375 mL) shredded
   aged Cheddar cheese
3 Tbsp (45 mL) chopped
   fresh cilantro
8 large (10-inch/25 cm) whole wheat
   flour tortillas
Optional toppings when serving:
   guacamole, salsa, sour cream, hot
   sauce, lettuce, tomato

Combine the water and quinoa in a medium saucepan. Bring to a boil, reduce to a simmer and cook, covered, for 15 minutes. Remove from the heat, uncover and set aside to cool completely.

Combine the paprika, cumin, chili powder, coriander, black pepper, onion powder, garlic powder and dried oregano in a small bowl. Set aside.

Heat the oil in a wide-bottomed saucepan over low heat. Add the onion and cook until transparent, 5 to 7 minutes. Stir in the seasoning you made and heat for 30 seconds. Add the quinoa, refried beans, Cheddar cheese and cilantro. Stir, then remove from the heat and cover.

Heat a 10-inch (25 cm) skillet on low, and gently warm each tortilla for a few seconds before wrapping burrito. Off the heat, scoop ¾ cup (175 mL) of filling onto one side of a tortilla. Starting from the filling side, fold in sides and tightly roll into a bundle. Set aside and repeat with the remaining ingredients.

Increase the heat under the skillet to medium. Place a burrito seam side down in the heated dry skillet. When golden brown, turn to the other side until it too is golden brown. Remove from the heat and repeat with the remaining burritos you want to eat immediately. Serve with desired toppings.

Freeze unheated burritos individually in plastic wrap or parchment paper, and place in a resealable plastic bag. Store in the freezer for up to 2 months. Thaw in the refrigerator overnight or in the microwave oven on high for 2 minutes per side. Warm and brown in a hot skillet over medium heat until golden on each side. Serve immediately with desired toppings.

CAULIFLOWER PIZZA CRUST

This pizza crust is crispy on the edges yet tender in the centre. It has a buttery flavour that provides a perfect backdrop for your favourite pizza toppings and is so easy to make—you won't ever have to wait for pizza dough to rise again. Other cauliflower crusts can be overloaded with even more cheese inside the crust, but we're giving you the option to add it on top, along with whatever additional toppings you love.

Serves 4 **GF**

4½ cups (1.1 L) cauliflower florets
½ cup (125 mL) grated Pecorino Romano cheese
2 large eggs, beaten
Your favourite pizza toppings

Preheat the oven to 450°F (230°C). Line a 12-inch (30 cm) pizza dish or pan with parchment paper and set aside.

Place the cauliflower in a food processor and process until mixture is very fine. Add the Pecorino Romano cheese and eggs and continue to blend until well combined.

Place the cauliflower mixture onto the pan and use your hands to spread and press it out evenly. Add your pizza toppings and bake for 25 to 30 minutes or until the edges of the crust are golden.

> TIP: 1. Add quinoa! If you have cooked quinoa on hand, add 2 Tbsp (30 mL) to your dough mixture for even more nutrition. 2. Wrap it up! Thin crusts make superb wraps! Form the dough into two or three 8-inch (20 cm) rounds and bake for 15 to 20 minutes. 3. Can't find Pecorino Romano cheese? Substitute with Parmesan cheese.

RED PEPPER AND BLACK OLIVE CAULIFLOWER PIZZA

Crispy yet tender cauliflower pizza crust is topped with a slightly spicy sauce, red pepper strips, black olives and a light sprinkle of mozzarella cheese for a dramatic and lively flavour combination. Serve it with the Mighty Mediterranean Minestrone (page 75).

Serves 4 **GF**

1 unbaked Cauliflower Pizza Crust (page 128)
1 Tbsp (15 mL) Sriracha hot sauce
1 Tbsp (15 mL) olive oil
1 cup (250 mL) sliced red bell pepper
¼ cup (60 mL) sliced black olives
⅓ cup (75 mL) shredded mozzarella cheese

Preheat the oven to 450°F (230°C). Prepare the pizza crust and set aside (do not bake).

In a small bowl, combine the hot sauce and oil. Lightly brush onto the crust surface, and top with red pepper and black olive slices. Sprinkle with mozzarella cheese. Bake for 25 to 30 minutes or until the edges of the crust are golden.

> TIP: Prefer thin crust? Simply reduce the Cauliflower Pizza Crust recipe by half and reduce the baking time to 15 to 20 minutes or until the edges are crisp and golden.

MUSHROOM AND CARAMELIZED ONION PIZZA WITH BRIE AND MAPLE

We love this slightly indulgent combination of a light garlic and Parmesan sauce, topped with caramelized onions, mushrooms and chunks of brie, finished with a drizzle of maple syrup. Not your everyday pizza, this is the perfect dish to whip up on a special occasion. Make this on a thick or thin Cauliflower Pizza Crust (page 128) or any of your own favourite crusts or flatbreads. Try this pizza alongside the Roasted Butternut Squash and Apple Soup with Crisp and Smoky Croutons (page 70).

Serves 4 GF

1 unbaked Cauliflower Pizza Crust (page 128)
1 Tbsp (15 mL) grapeseed oil or butter
1 cup (250 mL) white or yellow onion slices
2 cups (500 mL) sliced mushrooms (cremini, portobello or any mushrooms of your choice)
1 Tbsp (15 mL) unsalted butter
1 Tbsp (15 mL) rice flour, cornstarch or tapioca starch
½ cup (125 mL) 1% milk
½ tsp (2 mL) minced garlic
2 Tbsp (30 mL) grated Parmesan cheese
Pinch of sea salt
Pinch of ground black pepper
¼ cup (60 mL) sliced brie cheese
1 Tbsp (15 mL) pure maple syrup

Preheat the oven to 450°F (230°C). Prepare the pizza crust and set aside (do not bake).

Combine the oil and onion in a large saucepan over medium heat. Cook until the onion begins to soften and turn translucent, about 4 to 5 minutes. Add the mushrooms and continue to cook until softened, about 3 to 4 minutes. Set aside.

Melt butter in a medium saucepan over medium heat and add the flour. Whisk in the milk, continuing to stir until a smooth mixture is achieved. Add the garlic and Parmesan cheese and stir until thickened. Season with salt and pepper.

Spread this sauce on top of the unbaked pizza crust. Add the caramelized onion, mushrooms and slices of brie cheese. Bake for 25 to 30 minutes or until the edges of the crust are golden. Remove from the oven and drizzle with the maple syrup. Slice and serve hot.

CARAMELIZED ONION
WITH GRUYÈRE AND SAUERKRAUT ON DARK RYE

Once you try this gourmet sandwich, you will wonder why you didn't make yourself two! If you don't like sauerkraut, this is the sandwich that will change your mind. (True story for Carolyn!) This recipe makes for a quick lunch or light supper if you prepare the onions and sauce in advance. Serve this sandwich with the easy homemade Refrigerator Dill Pickles (page 201).

Makes 4

3 Tbsp (45 mL) unsalted butter
2 cups (500 mL) yellow onion, cut
   into slices ½ inch (1 cm) thick
Sea salt, to taste
⅓ cup (75 mL) Creamy Mayonnaise
   (page 197) or store-bought
1 Tbsp (15 mL) Tomato Ketchup
   (page 196) or store-bought
1 Tbsp (15 mL) relish
Pinch of pepper
8 slices of dark rye bread
4 large slices of Gruyère cheese
   (approximately 3½ oz/100 g)
1 cup (250 mL) prepared sauerkraut

Heat a large skillet on low heat and melt the butter. Stir in the onion and a pinch of salt and cover. Cook for approximately 20 minutes, stirring occasionally. Remove the lid and continue to cook and stir occasionally for another 20 minutes or until the onion is soft and translucent. Remove from the heat and set aside to cool.

Mix the mayonnaise, ketchup and relish in a small bowl. Season with salt and pepper, to taste. Set aside.

Toast 2 pieces of bread and spread 1 Tbsp (15 mL) of sauce on each piece. Place 1 slice of Gruyère cheese on 1 slice of the toasted bread, along with a scoop of sauerkraut and caramelized onion. Top with the remaining piece of toasted bread. Cut in half if desired and serve immediately. Repeat with remaining ingredients.

OPEN-FACED ARTICHOKE AND MUSHROOM BLT

Not your momma's BLT, this *bean*, lettuce and tomato beauty is light and lovely with a creamy purée of basil-infused white beans and tangy artichoke hearts, topped with the earthy-flavoured porcini mushrooms. These elevated flavours bring this sandwich to the next level.

Serves 10 to 12 **DF** **V**

1 oz (30 g) dried porcini mushrooms

1 can (19 oz/540 mL) white kidney beans, rinsed

1 can (14 oz/398 mL) artichoke hearts, drained

¼ cup (60 mL) chopped fresh basil

2 Tbsp (30 mL) extra virgin olive oil

2 tsp (10 mL) minced garlic

1 Tbsp (15 mL) fresh lemon juice

¼ tsp (1 mL) sea salt

1 to 2 whole wheat or white baguettes, sliced into rounds

12 to 15 lettuce or spinach leaves

3 Roma tomatoes, sliced ⅛ to ¼ inch (3 to 5 mm) thick

1 tsp (5 mL) za'atar (optional, see Tip on page 51)

Place the mushrooms in ¼ cup (60 mL) of water and set aside to rehydrate for 30 minutes. Strain the mushrooms and reserve the liquid.

Place the beans, artichokes, basil, oil, garlic, lemon juice, salt and the liquid from rehydrating the mushrooms in a blender or food processor. Purée until smooth. Spread the purée on slices of baguette, top with spinach, tomato slices and a few rehydrated mushrooms. Top each BLT with a pinch of flavourful za'atar (if using).

GLUTEN-FREE OPTION Replace the baguettes with gluten-free baguettes.

RAW OPTION Replace the baguettes with romaine hearts, the canned beans with raw, soaked or sprouted beans and the canned artichokes with raw artichokes.

PILED-HIGH JERK SANDWICHES

Our spicy Jamaican Jerk Tofu (page 149) is the perfect sandwich base. Pile these sandwiches with this delicious, aromatic mixture, and add some wonderful toppings: buttery avocado, smoky mayonnaise and creamy Havarti. This really is just as good, if not better, than its meaty cousin! Plate this with the delicious Superslaw (page 104).

Serves 4 to 6

1 batch Jamaican Jerk Tofu
  (page 149), not yet grilled
⅓ cup (75 mL) Creamy Mayonnaise
  (page 197) or store-bought
Pinch of smoked paprika or
  smoky pepper
4 to 6 whole-grain buns, halved
6 lettuce leaves
6 tomato slices
¼ cup (60 mL) sliced red onion
4 to 6 slices of Havarti cheese
1 avocado, peeled, pitted and sliced

Preheat the barbecue to 400°F (200°C). Oil the grill with a clean cloth. Place the tofu pieces on the grill, and cook for 3 to 4 minutes on each side until heated through, with crispy edges and grill marks. Set aside.

Stir the mayonnaise and paprika in a small bowl and set aside.

Heat the buns in a dry pan or on the grill until hot. Spread 1 Tbsp (15 mL) of the mayonnaise mixture between the top and bottom of each bun. Place the lettuce, tomato and onion on the bottoms, then add a Jerk patty. Top with Havarti cheese and then avocado. Finish with the tops of the toasted buns. Serve immediately.

GLUTEN-FREE OPTION Replace the buns with gluten-free buns.

TIP: For an alternative to the barbecue, fry the tofu on the stovetop in 1 Tbsp (15 mL) of oil over medium heat for about 3 minutes on each side, until golden. Or bake in a single layer on a parchment-lined baking sheet in a preheated 450°F (230°C) oven, for 5 to 7 minutes or until the edges are golden on each side.

HOT BARBECUE VEGGIE AND SUPERSLAW SANDWICHES

Look beyond barbecued pulled pork or beef sandwiches and try barbecued veggie sandwiches—you won't be disappointed! Our teenagers were in disbelief at how delicious these sandwiches are, and they've become a quick family favourite. If you're short on time, grating the vegetables is just fine. Crispy Baked Onion Rings with Tangy Dipping Sauce (page 52) or the Lazy Layered Salad with Herbed Kefir Ranch Dressing (page 102) make worthy sides.

Serves 4 to 6 **DF** **V**

6 cups (1.5 L) matchstick
   carrots or zucchini,
   or 3 cups (750 mL) of each
2 Tbsp (30 mL) water
1 cup (250 mL) prepared
   barbecue sauce
6 soft whole-grain buns, halved
1 batch Superslaw (page 104)

Heat a large saucepan over medium-low heat. Place the carrots in the saucepan and cover with the water. Cover and let simmer for 4 minutes. Stir in the zucchini (if using) and let simmer for another 3 minutes. Remove from the heat when the vegetables are tender-crisp, not mushy. Stir in the barbecue sauce and heat until hot.

Toast the buns. Place the barbecued vegetables (about ½ cup/125 mL) on each bun, topped with a scoop of slaw. Serve immediately.

GUACAMOLE PORTOBELLO BURGERS
WITH MISO BARBECUE SAUCE

How could you *not* love a thick, steak-like slab of meaty portobello mushroom, grilled and smothered with cheese, topped with creamy guacamole and a touch of hot and spicy miso barbecue sauce? Searing or charring from using a grill, barbecue or cast-iron skillet is what helps to give these mushrooms a smoky, fire-roasted flavour. Charred Corn and Roasted Vegetable Summer Salad with Peaches and Lime Herbed Buttermilk Dressing (page 108) or Za'atar Dusted Veggie Fries (page 51) make delicious sides!

Serves 4

MISO BARBECUE SAUCE
1 Tbsp (15 mL) sodium-reduced red miso
1 Tbsp (15 mL) Sriracha hot sauce
1½ Tbsp (22 mL) pure maple syrup
1 tsp (5 mL) soy sauce
1 tsp (5 mL) apple cider vinegar

GUACAMOLE PORTOBELLO BURGERS
½ cup (125 mL) raw, white onion rings
4 large portobello mushroom caps, washed and stems removed
4 slices of Monterey Jack cheese
4 large whole-grain burger buns
¼ cup (60 mL) guacamole
4 tomato slices

Whisk together the miso, hot sauce, maple syrup, soy sauce and vinegar in a small bowl. Set aside.

Preheat an outdoor barbecue, a large cast-iron skillet or a grill pan over medium heat. Grill the onion rings (use a vegetable tray if on a barbecue) until crispy brown and caramelized. Set aside.

Place the whole mushroom caps on the grill, top side up and baste with miso barbecue sauce. Grill or cook 3 to 4 minutes per side until the mushrooms are tender and the edges are seared. Baste one last time and top each mushroom first with a slice of cheese and then with the caramelized onion rings, continuing to cook for 1 minute more. Remove the mushrooms from the pan or grill and place each on a bun, along with 1 Tbsp (15 mL) of guacamole and a slice of tomato.

DAIRY-FREE OPTION Replace the Monterey Jack cheese with soy, nut or seed cheese or other dairy-free cheese.

GLUTEN-FREE OPTION Use gluten-free miso, replace the buns with gluten-free buns and replace the soy sauce with gluten-free tamari.

VEGAN OPTION Replace the Monterey Jack cheese with soy, nut or seed cheese or other vegan cheese.

> TIP: Make your own guacamole! Simply mash the flesh of 2 ripe avocados, and combine with 1 chopped tomato and 2 Tbsp (30 mL) each of finely chopped onion, lime juice, chopped cilantro, 1 tsp (5 mL) of garlic and a pinch of sea salt.

CHEESY VEGGIE JOES

Veggie Joes are a great option for a weeknight meal and are anything but sloppy! Make the filling ahead, then assemble quickly before serving. Patricia's teenagers love to prepare these on hectic weekdays because it's as easy as baking a frozen pizza but a whole lot more nutritious. Dinner is even more delicious when you serve this dish with Crispy Baked Onion Rings with Tangy Dipping Sauce (page 52) or the Lazy Layered Salad with Herbed Kefir Ranch Dressing (page 102).

Serves 4 to 6

2 Tbsp (30 mL) grapeseed oil
1 cup (250 mL) diced yellow onion
1 lb (450 g) mushrooms,
   coarsely chopped
1 green pepper,
   coarsely chopped
1 red pepper, coarsely chopped
1 can (14 oz/398 mL) plain
   tomato sauce
1 tsp (5 mL) Worcestershire sauce
   (vegan)
1 tsp (5 mL) paprika
½ tsp (2 mL) sea salt
¼ tsp (1 mL) dry mustard
¼ tsp (1 mL) ground black pepper
4 whole-grain buns, halved
1½ cups (375 mL) shredded
   mozzarella cheese

Preheat the oven to 350°F (180°C).

Heat the oil in a large-bottomed saucepan on medium-low heat. Cover and cook until the onion is translucent, about 5 minutes. Stir in the mushrooms and peppers. Cover again and cook until the vegetables are tender, about 4 to 6 minutes. Stir in the tomato sauce, Worcestershire, paprika, salt, mustard and pepper, and simmer, uncovered, until the sauce reduces and becomes thick, about 4 to 5 minutes. At this point, you can refrigerate the mixture in a resealable container until assembly.

When ready to assemble, place the bun halves face side up on a baking sheet. Scoop about ½ cup (125 mL) of the veggie joes mixture on each bun. Top each with mozzarella cheese and bake until cheese is melted and golden. Serve immediately.

GLUTEN-FREE OPTION Use gluten-free Worcestershire sauce and replace the whole-grain buns with gluten-free buns.

GRILLED PINEAPPLE TERIYAKI BURGERS

Who needs meat when this delicious vegetarian version includes marinated teriyaki tofu topped with sweet, grilled and caramelized pineapple over melted jalapeño Havarti cheese, crisp onions and lettuce on a toasted bun. The cheese adds a different element of creaminess, with a hint of heat along with the sweet and tangy flavours. We love to serve these burgers with Baked Eggplant Chips with Lime Miso Yogurt Dip (page 46) or you may want to try the Spicy Quinoa Fries with Ginger Carrot Dip (page 45).

Serves 4 to 6

TERIYAKI BURGERS

1 package (12 oz/350 g) extra-firm tofu, sliced in half across the narrow middle and then sliced into 6 square patties about 3 inches (7.5 cm) wide

1 can (14 oz/398 mL) unsweetened pineapple rings, juice reserved

6 whole-grain buns

6 lettuce leaves

6 slices of jalapeño Havarti, regular Havarti or Farmers cheese

6 red onion rings, ¼ inch (5 mm) thick

¼ cup (60 mL) Creamy Mayonnaise (page 197) or store-bought (optional)

MARINADE

½ cup (125 mL) reserved pineapple juice

½ cup (125 mL) soy sauce

½ cup (125 mL) liquid honey

2 Tbsp (30 mL) minced garlic

2 Tbsp (30 mL) sesame oil

2 tsp (10 mL) sesame seeds

1 tsp (5 mL) grated fresh ginger

½ tsp (2 mL) dried chili flakes

2 tsp (10 mL) cornstarch

Place the tofu in a single layer on a cutting board wrapped in a clean kitchen towel. Place something flat and heavy on top of the tofu, such as a large cast-iron pot or skillet. Set aside to press the tofu for 1 hour or longer. Place the tofu in a single layer in a 13- × 9-inch (3.5 L) baking dish.

Whisk the pineapple juice, soy sauce, honey, garlic, oil, sesame seeds, grated ginger and dried chili flakes in a small bowl. Pour over the tofu, making sure the marinade touches all sides of the tofu. Marinate for 1 hour, turning the tofu after 30 minutes.

Pour the marinade into a small saucepan over medium-low heat and whisk in the cornstarch. Stir frequently and allow mixture to reduce until it is thick enough to coat the back of a spoon. Remove from the heat and set aside.

Preheat the barbecue to approximately 350°F (180°C). Oil the grill lightly with a clean cloth. Place the tofu on the grill and cook 5 to 7 minutes per side or until each side is hot, has grill marks and has brown, caramelized edges. Barbecue the pineapple rings until hot and caramelized with grill marks. Remove from the grill and place on a plate before assembly.

Toast the buns for a minute or two on the grill until lightly toasted. Assemble the burger by first spreading some of the reduced marinade on the bottom of the bun. Then top with a lettuce leaf, a tofu patty, a Havarti cheese slice, a barbecued pineapple ring and a red onion ring. Spread the top bun with the mayonnaise (if using). Serve immediately.

DAIRY-FREE OPTION Replace the cheese with soy, nut, seed or other dairy-free cheese.

GLUTEN-FREE OPTION Replace the soy sauce with gluten-free tamari and replace the whole-grain buns with gluten-free buns.

VEGAN OPTION Replace the honey with pure maple syrup, the cheese with soy, nut, seed or other vegan cheese and the mayonnaise with vegan mayonnaise.

BAKED DISHES, CASSEROLES AND ONE-POT MEALS

SWEET CORN AND FENNEL SUCCOTASH CASSEROLE

We love this full-flavoured succotash. Red pepper, sweet corn, fennel, green and black beans are gently sautéed with onions, garlic and vegetable broth and then baked in a light and creamy sauce packed with garden-fresh herbs. A crispy, golden topping of panko breadcrumbs and Parmesan cheese tricks out this summer dish, giving it a comfort food feel without the high calories.

Serves 4 to 6

1 Tbsp (15 mL) grapeseed oil

1 cup (250 mL) chopped white or yellow onion

2 tsp (10 mL) minced garlic

3 cups (750 mL) fresh or frozen sweet corn kernels

1 cup (250 mL) chopped red bell pepper

1 cup (250 mL) sliced fresh or frozen green beans

1 cup (250 mL) canned or cooked black beans

1½ cups (375 mL) thinly sliced fennel

¾ cup (175 mL) Simple Vegetable Broth (page 62) or low-sodium, store-bought vegetable broth

2½ Tbsp (37 mL) chopped fresh basil

2½ Tbsp (37 mL) chopped fresh parsley

⅔ cup (150 mL) Natural Plain Yogurt (page 195) or store-bought

1 large egg, lightly beaten

Sea salt and ground black pepper, to taste

½ cup (125 mL) panko breadcrumbs

½ cup (125 mL) grated Parmesan cheese

Preheat the oven to 350°F (180°C). Lightly spray with cooking oil or grease a 13- × 9-inch (3.5 L) baking dish and set aside.

Combine the oil and onion in a large saucepan over medium heat. Cook until the onion begins to soften and turn translucent, about 4 to 5 minutes. Reduce the heat to medium-low and add the garlic, corn, red pepper, both beans, fennel and broth. Cover and steam the mixture for 4 to 6 minutes or until the green beans are lightly cooked and crisp and no broth remains in the pan. (Remove the lid to reduce if necessary.) Allow the mixture to cool slightly and add the basil, parsley, yogurt and egg. Season with salt and pepper. Mix together and gently pack mixture into the prepared baking dish. Set aside.

Combine the panko and Parmesan cheese in a small bowl, and sprinkle evenly over the top of the casserole. Bake for 20 to 22 minutes or until the topping is crispy.

GLUTEN-FREE OPTION Replace the panko breadcrumbs with gluten-free breadcrumbs.

EGGS MORNAY OVER TENDER ASPARAGUS AND PORTOBELLO

Eggs are a superb protein source and make great meatless meals. Eggs Mornay is reminiscent of the Benedict version, but without the English muffin. Instead it has a grilled tomato layered with tender portobello and asparagus, topped with an egg and a tangy rich Gruyère cheese sauce. Although this recipe is absolutely divine in the morning, we also highly recommend it for dinner! If you don't require gluten-free, you can use all-purpose flour instead of rice flour.

Serves 4 **GF**

CHEESE SAUCE
3 Tbsp (45 mL) grapeseed oil
  or butter
2 Tbsp (30 mL) rice flour
¼ tsp (1 mL) dry mustard
¼ tsp (1 mL) sea salt
1 cup (250 mL) warm milk or
  non-dairy milk
¾ cup (175 mL) grated Gruyère
  cheese

4 portobello or 8 mini portobello
  mushrooms
2 Tbsp (30 mL) olive oil, divided
¾ lb (340 g) asparagus, tough ends
  trimmed and halved
½ tsp (2 mL) minced garlic
Pinch of sea salt
2 tsp (10 mL) fresh lemon juice
2 large beefsteak tomatoes, cut into
  slices ¼ inch (5 mm) thick
8 large eggs
2 Tbsp (30 mL) thinly sliced
  fresh chives
½ tsp (2 mL) ground black pepper

Preheat the oven to 325°F (160°C).

Heat a small saucepan on medium-low heat. Stir in the grapeseed oil and flour. Allow the mixture to cook for approximately 30 seconds. Add the mustard and salt, heating for another 10 seconds. Whisk in the warm milk until it starts to thicken and coats the back of a spoon. Stir in the Gruyère cheese until melted. Turn off the heat and cover. Set aside.

Heat a Dutch oven or wide-bottomed saucepan on medium-low heat. Add ⅓ cup (75 mL) of water to the pan. Place the mushrooms top side down in the pan. Cover and cook for 7 minutes or until tender. Remove from the pan and place in a 13- × 9-inch (3.5 L) baking dish. Cover with foil. Place the baking dish in the oven to keep warm.

Return the saucepan to the burner. Heat 1 Tbsp (15 mL) of olive oil in the saucepan over medium-low heat. Add the asparagus. Cook for about 4 minutes. Stir in the garlic and salt. Cook, covered, until tender-crisp. Drizzle with the lemon juice. Place the asparagus in the baking dish with the mushrooms, cover and return to the oven.

Again return the saucepan to the burner. Heat the remaining 1 Tbsp (15 mL) of olive oil in the saucepan over medium heat. Add the tomatoes. Fry each side until hot, about 3 minutes. Set aside.

Clean and heat the saucepan over medium-high heat. Brush with oil. Fry the eggs sunny side up. Plate immediately, first placing one slice of tomato, then a large mushroom (cap side down) on each plate. Top with eggs (two for large portobello, one for each smaller portobello), then place the asparagus across the eggs. Top with cheese sauce, a sprinkle of chives and pepper. Serve immediately.

MAPLE AND SUMAC BAKED BEANS

We love this slow-cooked dish, and how the wonderful flavours of sautéed onions, tomato, molasses, maple syrup, cayenne pepper and woodsy, lemony sumac are infused into these comforting, nourishing beans. When cooked, the beans are thick and not overly saucy—so if you prefer a lot of sauce, double everything but the beans!

Serves 6 to 8 **DF** **V**

4 cups (1 L) dry white
    navy beans
1 Tbsp (15 mL) grapeseed oil or
    vegetable oil
1 cup (250 mL) chopped
    white onion
4 cups (1 L) Simple Vegetable Broth
    (page 62) or low-sodium, store-
    bought vegetable broth
¼ cup (60 mL) tomato paste
⅓ cup (75 mL) pure maple syrup
⅓ cup (75 mL) fancy molasses
1 Tbsp (15 mL) Worcestershire sauce
    (vegan)
2 tsp (10 mL) ground sumac
1 tsp (5 mL) sea salt
½ tsp (2 mL) ground black pepper
¼ tsp (1 mL) cayenne pepper

Place the beans in a large bowl with water, ensuring all beans are covered. Refrigerate and soak overnight. Once rehydrated, remove the beans from the refrigerator, rinse and set aside.

Preheat the oven to 350°F (180°C). Place the oil and onion in a large oven-safe saucepan or Dutch oven over medium heat, and cook for about 5 minutes or until softened. Stir in the broth, tomato paste, maple syrup, molasses and Worcestershire.

Add the beans to the mixture and bring to a boil for 5 minutes. Remove from the heat and add the sumac, salt, black pepper and cayenne pepper and mix well. Cover and bake for 3 to 3½ hours until the beans are cooked through and soft. Store for up to 1 week in the refrigerator or freeze for up to 2 months.

GLUTEN-FREE OPTION Use gluten-free Worcestershire sauce.

> TIP: Don't have white navy beans? Any small white beans can be substituted here. Try white kidney (cannellini), pinto or great northern beans.

JAMAICAN JERK TOFU

Our savoury, sweet and spicy marinated tofu is accented with the classic Caribbean flavours of allspice, ginger, lime, thyme and a hint of cinnamon. It pairs beautifully with our Caribbean Coconut and Black Bean Quinoa (page 57) or Superslaw (page 104).

Serves 4 to 6 DF GF

1 package (12 oz/350 g)
   extra-firm tofu
4 green scallions, coarsely chopped
1 scotch bonnet or jalapeño pepper
¼ cup (60 mL) fresh lime juice
¼ cup (60 mL) olive oil
3 Tbsp (45 mL) liquid honey
2 Tbsp (30 mL) grated fresh ginger
1 Tbsp (15 mL) dried thyme
1 tsp (5 mL) minced garlic
½ tsp (2 mL) ground allspice
¼ tsp (1 mL) sea salt
¼ tsp (1 mL) cinnamon
Pinch of ground black pepper

Slice the tofu into 2- to 3-inch (5 to 7.5 cm) squares, and slice each square into 3 patties. Place the tofu in a single layer on a cutting board wrapped in a clean towel. Place something flat and heavy on top of the tofu, such as a large cast-iron pot or skillet, for at least 30 minutes. Place the tofu pieces in single layer in a 13- × 9-inch (3.5 L) baking dish.

Place the scallions, scotch bonnet, lime juice, oil, honey, ginger, thyme, garlic, allspice, salt, cinnamon and pepper in a blender. Purée until smooth and pour over the tofu, ensuring all sides are coated. Marinate for 1 hour (or overnight), turning the pieces over at the halfway point.

Preheat a barbecue to 400°F (200°C). Oil the grill with a clean cloth. Place the tofu pieces directly on the grill and cook for 3 to 4 minutes on each side until heated, with crispy edges and grill marks. Remove from the heat and serve.

VEGAN OPTION Replace the honey with pure maple syrup.

> TIP: 1. **To Cook Tofu in the Oven** Preheat the oven to 450°F (230°C). Bake marinated tofu in a single layer on a parchment-lined baking sheet for 5 to 7 minutes until the edges are golden on each side. 2. **To Cook Tofu on the Stovetop** Place the marinated tofu in a skillet with 1 Tbsp (15 mL) of oil over medium heat, and cook for about 3 minutes per side, until golden.

PARMESAN PETAL SKILLET RATATOUILLE OVER ANCIENT GRAINS

Traditional ratatouille recipes can be complicated and time consuming, which makes it difficult to prepare on most weekdays. So here's our version, three ways—skillet, slow cooker and oven—whichever suits your schedule. Herbs de Provence are a simple way to incorporate multiple flavours in one easy step. With the time you've saved, make the delicious goat cheese toasts that accompany this dish—you won't regret it!

Serves 4 to 6

1⅓ cups (325 mL) water
⅓ cup (75 mL) quinoa
⅓ cup (75 mL) millet
2 Tbsp (30 mL) grapeseed oil
¾ cup (175 mL) chopped onion
½ tsp (2 mL) sea salt
2 Tbsp (30 mL) minced garlic
2 tsp (10 mL) herbs de Provence
12 oz (350 g) eggplant or 2 small
    eggplants (peel if desired)
1 lb (450 g) zucchini, diced
1 red bell pepper, seeds removed
    and diced large
1 green bell pepper, seeds removed
    and diced large
1 can (28 oz/796 mL) diced
    tomatoes
½ cup (125 mL) shaved Parmesan
    cheese petals
Freshly ground black pepper

OVEN-BAKED GOAT CHEESE TOASTS (OPTIONAL)

10 slices of artisan or
    French bread
4 oz (115 g) fresh unripened
    goat cheese

Bring the water, quinoa and millet to a boil in a medium saucepan. Cover and reduce to a simmer for 10 minutes. Remove from the heat and let sit, covered, for an additional 5 minutes.

In a skillet: Heat a deep skillet or Dutch oven over medium-low heat. Add the oil, onion and salt. Cook, covered, for about 5 minutes or until the onion becomes tender. Stir in the garlic and herbs de Provence, and cook for 1 minute more. Add the eggplant, zucchini and bell peppers, frying until the edges are golden, about 5 minutes. Stir in the tomatoes with the juice. Cover and cook for 8 to 10 minutes or until tender. Serve over cooked quinoa and millet and top with Parmesan cheese petals and pepper, to taste.

In a slow cooker: Heat a saucepan over medium-low heat. Add the oil, onion and salt, and cook until the onion starts to soften, about 5 minutes. Place the mixture in the slow cooker. Stir in the garlic, herbs de Provence, eggplant, zucchini, bell peppers and tomatoes (juice drained). Cook in the slow cooker on low for 4 to 6 hours. Serve over cooked quinoa and millet. Garnish with Parmesan cheese petals and pepper, to taste.

In the oven: Preheat the oven to 350°F (180°C). Heat a saucepan over medium-low heat. Add the oil, onion and salt, and cook until the onion starts to soften, about 5 minutes. Place in a large covered casserole. Stir in the garlic, herbs de Provence, eggplant, zucchini, bell peppers and tomatoes with the juice. Cook in oven for 2 hours. Serve over cooked quinoa and millet. Garnish with Parmesan cheese petals and pepper, to taste.

Prepare the Oven-Baked Goat Cheese Toasts (if using). Preheat the oven to 400°F (200°C) and line a baking sheet with parchment paper. Spread the goat cheese over the bread slices. Place the slices on the baking sheet, and bake until the edges are golden, 6 to 8 minutes. Serve the toasts and the ratatouille together, hot.

GLUTEN-FREE OPTION Use gluten-free artisan or French bread slices.

CORN AND EDAMAME
FRIED RED RICE STUFFED ZUCCHINI

This baked dish is definitely a change from your traditional stuffed pepper. A perfect dinner to be served in late summer or early fall, seasonal zucchini and corn are baked with a colourful and hearty red rice mixture that includes chewy edamame. Zesty and savoury, these stuffed beauties are loaded to thrill your taste buds with fresh cilantro, tangy lime, ginger and the exciting and unique lemony flavour of sumac spice. Cook the rice the day before you need it to reduce your final prep time.

Serves 4 **DF** **V**

1⅓ cups (325 mL) water

⅔ cup (150 mL) red heirloom rice, well rinsed

1 Tbsp (15 mL) grapeseed oil or sesame oil

⅓ cup (75 mL) chopped white or yellow onion

½ cup (125 mL) fresh or frozen shelled edamame

⅔ cup (150 mL) fresh or frozen corn kernels

1 Tbsp (15 mL) soy sauce

1 Tbsp (15 mL) fresh lime juice

1 tsp (5 mL) ground sumac

1 tsp (5 mL) pure maple syrup

1 tsp (5 mL) minced fresh ginger

2 Tbsp (30 mL) chopped fresh cilantro

2 large zucchini or 3 small/medium sized, cut lengthwise, seeds removed

Preheat the oven to 350°F (180°C). Line an 11- × 7-inch (2 L) baking dish with parchment paper and set aside.

Combine the water and the rice in a medium saucepan and bring to a boil. Reduce to a simmer and cook, covered, for 30 to 40 minutes or until water is completely absorbed and the rice is soft and fluffy.

Heat the oil in a large skillet on medium heat and add the onion, edamame and corn. Sauté until the onion is softened, about 4 to 5 minutes. Add the cooked rice, soy sauce and lime juice. Add the sumac, maple syrup and ginger, and continue to cook for 5 to 6 minutes or until the mixture is heated through. If the pan appears dry or the rice mixture sticks to the bottom, add 1 or 2 tsp (5 or 10 mL) of water. This will help bring all the yummy browned bits baked on the bottom of the pan back into the rice mixture.

Remove from the heat and toss in the cilantro. Stuff approximately ⅓ cup (75 mL) of rice mixture into each zucchini and place in the prepared baking dish. Cover with foil and bake for 30 to 35 minutes or until the zucchini is baked through. Serve warm.

GLUTEN-FREE OPTION Replace the soy sauce with gluten-free tamari.

SWEET MILLET AND CHICKPEA STUFFED PEPPERS WITH ROSEMARY AND PARMESAN

Take pleasure in eating a stuffed pepper as the main part of your meal or half as a side dish. The naturally subtle sweetness of the peppers, millet and chickpeas beautifully blend with the rosemary and red pepper flakes and the salty crispness of baked Parmesan cheese. If you don't have millet handy, this recipe works just as well with an equal amount of quinoa.

Serves 4 as a main or 8 as a side **GF**

4 sweet red, yellow or
   orange peppers
3 Tbsp (45 mL) grapeseed oil
2 tsp (10 mL) chopped fresh
   rosemary
1 tsp (5 mL) minced garlic
½ to 1 tsp (2 to 5 mL) crushed
   red pepper flakes
5 bay leaves, divided
2 cups (500 mL) Simple Vegetable
   Broth (page 62) or low-sodium,
   store-bought vegetable broth
   or water
1 cup (250 mL) millet
1 cup (250 mL) cooked chickpeas
½ cup (125 mL) grated Parmesan
   cheese, divided

Preheat the oven to 350°F (180°C). Line one 8-inch (2 L) square baking dish (for 4 peppers) or one 13- × 9-inch (3.5 L) baking dish with parchment paper.

Cut around the stem of each pepper and discard the seeds and stem. Place the peppers upright in a baking dish (trim the bottoms slightly to help them stand if necessary, or use a muffin tin) and set aside.

Heat the oil in a medium saucepan over medium-low heat. Add the rosemary, garlic, red pepper flakes and 1 bay leaf, stirring and heating for about 30 seconds. Add the broth and millet. Bring to a boil, reduce the heat to a simmer and cover. Cook for 15 minutes. Stir in the chickpeas and ¼ cup (60 mL) of Parmesan cheese.

Spoon the filling into each of the peppers, filling any gaps or air pockets. Sprinkle each with 1 Tbsp (15 mL) of Parmesan cheese, tuck one bay leaf into each pepper and return each to the baking dish. Place in the oven uncovered and bake for 25 to 30 minutes or until peppers are tender and the cheese is golden. Remove from the oven and allow to cool for about 3 to 5 minutes before serving.

> TIP: Make as directed above but instead cut each pepper in half by slicing lengthwise and removing the seeds. This modification requires an additional ¼ cup (60 mL) of Parmesan cheese and 4 bay leaves and reduces the cooking time by approximately 5 minutes.

CHEESY CAULIFLOWER AND SWEET POTATO BAKE

Who doesn't love the combination of cauliflower and cheese? In our version of this well-known dish, tender-crisp cauliflower is baked in a thick and creamy Cheddar and sweet potato sauce, and topped with a tasty, crunchy pecan topping. This is delicious and filling comfort food at its best and also virtually guilt free. You're welcome! Serve it along with the Meatless Meatloaf (page 162) or the Pepper-Crusted Mushroom Steaks (page 160) for a king's feast. If you don't require gluten-free, you may use regular all-purpose flour instead of rice flour and any bread-crumbs you like.

Serves 4 to 6 **GF**

1 head cauliflower, cut into
  bite-sized pieces
1 cup (250 mL) shredded aged
  Cheddar cheese
1½ cups (375 mL) cooked and
  mashed sweet potato
1 cup (250 mL) milk or
  non-dairy milk
¼ cup (60 mL) rice flour
½ tsp (2 mL) dry mustard
½ tsp (2 mL) sea salt
¼ tsp (1 mL) ground black pepper
Dash of hot sauce (optional)
½ cup (125 mL) fine dry gluten-free
  bread crumbs
2 Tbsp (30 mL) finely
  chopped pecans
1 Tbsp (15 mL) salted butter, melted

Preheat the oven to 375°F (190°C). Lightly grease six 2-cup (500 mL) ovenproof bowls or one 9-inch (2.5 L) square glass baking dish. Set aside.

Place the cauliflower pieces and Cheddar cheese in a large bowl and set aside. Purée the sweet potato, milk, flour, mustard, salt, black pepper and hot sauce (if using) in a blender. Pour over the cauliflower and Cheddar cheese. Fold until cauliflower is fully coated. Evenly divide between the ovenproof bowls or spread in the baking dish.

Mix the breadcrumbs, pecan pieces and butter in a small bowl. Sprinkle over the cauliflower mixture, and bake for 30 to 40 minutes or until the cauliflower is tender, the sauce is thick and bubbling and the bread-crumb topping is golden. Remove from the oven and let rest 5 minutes before serving.

SPICY FARRO ENCHILADAS WITH MONTEREY JACK CHEESE

Normally a fairly indulgent meal, enchiladas made at home are a complete game-changer. Say hello to fibre-packed ancient grains, beans and veggies you can customize, make the night before and pop in the oven when you're home from work. They're piquant and scrumptious, with tender tortillas wrapped around spiced-up farro, beans, corn, cheese and fresh cilantro, smothered in a tangy enchilada sauce. Don't have farro on hand? Use 1½ cups (375 mL) cooked quinoa, millet, freekeh or your favourite heirloom rice instead.

Serves 4

½ cup (125 mL) farro

1¼ cups (300 mL) water

1 cup (250 mL) chipotle peppers in adobo sauce

½ cup (125 mL) chopped white or yellow onion

2 tsp (10 mL) minced garlic

1 cup (250 mL) tomato sauce

1 Tbsp (15 mL) brown sugar

½ tsp (2 mL) cumin

Sea salt and ground black pepper, to taste

¾ cup (175 mL) canned black beans, drained and rinsed, or cooked black beans

½ cup (125 mL) fresh or frozen corn kernels

1⅓ cups (325 mL) shredded Monterey Jack cheese, divided

¼ cup (60 mL) chopped fresh cilantro

10 medium (8-inch/20 cm) Whole Wheat Soft Flour Tortillas (page 117) or store-bought whole wheat flour tortillas

1 Tbsp (15 mL) grapeseed oil

Sour cream or plain Greek yogurt, for serving

Preheat the oven to 350°F (180°C). Line a 13- × 9-inch (3.5 L) baking pan with parchment paper and set aside.

Combine the farro and water in a medium saucepan, cover and bring to a boil. Reduce the heat and simmer for about 25 to 30 minutes or until the farro is soft and chewy and no water remains. (Drain any excess water after farro is cooked.) Set aside.

Purée the chipotle peppers and adobo sauce along with the onion and garlic in a small food processor or blender. In a medium saucepan, combine the chipotle pepper purée with the tomato sauce, sugar, cumin, salt and pepper over low heat. Simmer until heated through. Combine the cooked farro, beans, corn, ¾ cup (175 mL) of Monterey Jack cheese, cilantro and 1 cup (250 mL) of the chipotle tomato sauce in a medium bowl and mix well.

Place the tortillas on a flat work surface, and scoop 3 Tbsp (45 mL) of the farro filling into the centre of each tortilla. (If the tortillas are stiff, place them in the oven for 1 to 2 minutes to warm first.) Roll each, folding in the ends of the tortilla to keep the filling from falling out. Place the enchiladas seam side down in the prepared baking pan. Lightly brush with the oil, cover in the remaining chipotle sauce and sprinkle with the remaining Monterey Jack cheese.

Bake for 10 to 12 minutes or until the cheese is bubbling and the edges begin to brown. Serve hot with a dollop of sour cream or Greek yogurt.

GLUTEN-FREE OPTION Replace the farro with quinoa and use gluten-free tortillas.

PORCINI-BREADED TOFU RED RICE BOWL

Maybe you've never eaten tofu or you're not a big fan? Well, this recipe may change your mind. Extra-firm tofu is cubed and absorbs a spicy marinade of garlic, ginger and Sriracha, then is breaded in ground dried porcini mushrooms and pan-fried until golden. Served on top of a bed of floral-scented heirloom red rice and topped with crunchy peanuts and fresh cilantro, this dish might just make you crave tofu.

Serves 4 **DF**

1 package (12 oz/350 g) extra-firm tofu

½ cup (125 mL) soy sauce

¼ cup (60 mL) Sriracha hot sauce

1 Tbsp (15 mL) grated fresh ginger

2 tsp (10 mL) minced garlic

1 oz (30 g) dried porcini mushrooms

1 cup (250 mL) red heirloom rice

2½ cups (625 mL) Simple Vegetable Broth (page 62) or low-sodium, store-bought vegetable broth

½ cup (125 mL) chopped fresh cilantro

3 to 4 Tbsp (45 to 60 mL) grapeseed oil

4 large eggs

¼ cup (60 mL) roasted, chopped, unsalted peanuts

2 Tbsp (30 mL) sliced green onion (greens only)

Dice the tofu into bite-sized pieces and place on paper towels to remove any excess moisture. Set aside.

Whisk the soy sauce, hot sauce, ginger and garlic in a medium bowl, and add the tofu chunks. Ensure all the tofu is coated in sauce and set aside for 30 minutes while you prepare the rest of the recipe. Grind the dried mushrooms in a spice grinder or coffee grinder (or even a small food processor, sifting and repeatedly grinding any larger chunks) and set aside.

Rinse the rice under cold water until the water runs clear. Place the rice and broth in a medium saucepan and bring to a boil. Reduce to a simmer and cook, covered, for 30 to 35 minutes or until rice is soft and all the broth is absorbed. Mix in the cilantro and set aside to keep warm.

Place the oil in a medium skillet or frying pan over medium-high heat. Toss each piece of tofu in the ground mushrooms and place in the skillet. Brown all sides of the tofu until golden, approximately 4 to 5 minutes. Set aside and keep warm.

Just before serving, poach the eggs (or fry if you prefer). Divide the rice equally between 4 serving bowls and top with tofu chunks and eggs. Sprinkle with peanuts and green onion.

GLUTEN-FREE OPTION Replace the soy sauce with gluten-free tamari.

> TIP: Want to add another flavour dimension? Top each serving with ¼ cup (60 mL) of kimchi.

PEPPER-CRUSTED MUSHROOM STEAKS

These steaks are mouth-watering, juicy, meaty and rich in flavour—but just happen to be mushrooms! We've concocted the perfect marinade. Soy sauce, balsamic vinegar, smoked paprika, garlic and freshly ground pepper make these large portobello mushroom steaks sing, thanks to the combination of salty, tangy and smoky flavours. Barbecuing adds another dimension, with a fire-grilled taste that will make you forget all about meat. Serve with the Za'atar Dusted Veggie Fries (page 51) for a complete meal.

Serves 4

½ cup (125 mL) olive oil
¼ cup (60 mL) soy sauce
¼ cup (60 mL) balsamic vinegar
2 shallots, chopped
2 Tbsp (30 mL) minced garlic
2 Tbsp (30 mL) dried basil
4 tsp (20 mL) dried parsley flakes
½ tsp (2 mL) freshly ground
    black pepper
¼ tsp (1 mL) smoked paprika
4 portobello mushrooms

Place the oil, soy sauce, vinegar, shallots, garlic, basil, parsley, pepper and paprika in a blender. Blend until the marinade is fully combined and the onion is puréed or minced. Place the mushrooms in a resealable plastic bag or marinating container. Pour the marinade over the mushrooms until completely covered. Let sit in the refrigerator for 1 hour or overnight.

Preheat a barbecue to approximately 400°F (200°C). Place the mushrooms onto the hot grill, cap side down. Barbecue for 8 minutes on each side or until the mushrooms are golden and the juices are releasing. Remove them from the grill and let sit for 3 minutes before serving.

GLUTEN-FREE OPTION Replace the soy sauce with gluten-free tamari.

> TIP: The mushroom steaks are wonderful when served with warm caramelized onions and room-temperature blue cheese, similar to a beef steak.

MEATLESS MEATLOAF

This winning meatloaf has a "beefy" appearance, but even better, its baked, crisp flavour will make you completely forget you're eating meatless! Red quinoa, pecans, mushrooms and oats provide the right texture and flavour, along with marjoram and oregano. Serve traditionally, alongside your favourite potato or root vegetable mash, like our Parsnip, Cauliflower and Potato Mash with Sage (page 49), green beans, Miso Mushroom Gravy (page 198) or any favourite gravy.

Serves 8

1 cup (250 mL) red or
    tricoloured quinoa
2 cups (500 mL) water
1 to 2 Tbsp (15 to 30 mL)
    grapeseed oil
1½ cups (375 mL) diced onion
3 cups (750 mL) chopped fresh
    cremini or white button
    mushrooms
2 tsp (10 mL) minced garlic
1¾ tsp (8 mL) dried marjoram
¾ tsp (3 mL) dried oregano
2 large eggs
1¼ cups (300 mL) shredded
    Cheddar cheese
¾ cup (175 mL) chopped,
    toasted pecans
⅔ cup (150 mL) quick-cooking oats
    or rolled oats
2 Tbsp (30 mL) soy sauce

Preheat the oven to 350°F (180°C). Lightly grease or spray with cooking oil one 8- × 4-inch (1.5 L) loaf pan, line with parchment paper and set aside.

Combine the quinoa and water in a large saucepan. Bring to a boil, reduce to a simmer, cover and cook for 15 minutes. Remove from the heat and let sit, covered, for another 10 minutes. Fluff with a fork and set aside to cool.

Heat the oil in a large saucepan over medium heat. Add the onion and cook for about 5 minutes, until it becomes soft and translucent. Add the mushrooms, garlic, marjoram and oregano, and cook for another 5 minutes or until the mushrooms are soft and tender. Set aside to cool. When cooled, place in a food processor and pulse until the mixture is finely chopped and well mixed. Set aside.

In a medium bowl, beat the eggs. Add the cooked quinoa, mushroom mixture, Cheddar cheese, pecans, oats and soy sauce. Scoop the mixture into the prepared loaf pan and press down firmly on top by using a piece of parchment paper or clean hands.

Bake for 35 to 40 minutes or until the surface is crispy and the inside is cooked through. Move to a wire rack to cool slightly. Slice while still warm and serve. Refrigerate and store for up to 4 days.

DAIRY-FREE OPTION Replace the Cheddar cheese with soy, nut or seed cheese or other dairy-free cheese.

GLUTEN-FREE OPTION Use gluten-free rolled or quick oats and replace the soy sauce with gluten-free tamari.

STEEL-CUT OAT SHEPHERD'S PIE WITH PARSNIP, CAULIFLOWER AND POTATO MASH WITH SAGE

Savoury cooked steel-cut oats and vegetables are the hearty, chunky base of this rich, meatless pie. Topped with whipped Parsnip, Cauliflower and Potato Mash with Sage (page 49), this dish is full of pleasing flavour and warm comfort.

Serves 6

1 Tbsp (15 mL) grapeseed oil

1 cup (250 mL) chopped white onion

2 cups (500 mL) sliced cremini mushrooms (or a mixture of cremini and portobello)

1½ cups (375 mL) sliced carrot

1 bay leaf

1 tsp (5 mL) minced garlic

1 cup (250 mL) steel-cut oats

4 cups (1 L) Simple Vegetable Broth (page 62) or low-sodium, store-bought vegetable broth

2 tsp (10 mL) red miso

1 Tbsp (15 mL) chopped fresh rosemary

1 Tbsp (15 mL) chopped fresh thyme

¼ tsp (1 mL) ground sage

½ tsp (2 mL) ground black pepper

Sea salt, to taste

½ cup (125 mL) fresh or frozen peas

½ cup (125 mL) fresh or frozen corn kernels

1 batch Parsnip, Cauliflower and Potato Mash with Sage (page 49)

Preheat the oven to 400°F (200°C) and set aside a 13- × 9-inch (3.5 L) baking dish.

Combine the oil and onion in a large saucepan over medium heat. Cook until the onion begins to soften and turn translucent, about 4 to 5 minutes. Add the mushrooms, carrot, bay leaf and garlic, and continue to cook until mushrooms have slightly softened, about 3 to 4 minutes. Add the steel-cut oats and broth. Cook for 25 to 30 minutes or until the oats are soft and tender. Halfway through the cooking time, stir in the miso, rosemary, thyme, sage, black pepper and salt. Add the peas and corn.

Spread the oat mixture evenly in the baking dish, and top with an even layer of the parsnip, cauliflower and potato mash. Place in the oven and bake for 25 to 30 minutes or until the edges are baked golden and the inside is piping hot.

GLUTEN-FREE OPTION Use gluten-free steel-cut oats and gluten-free miso.

> TIP: If you want to pipe your mashed potatoes on top (rather than spreading them on with a spatula), make double the amount of Parsnip, Cauliflower and Potato Mash with Sage (page 49). This will give the dish a stunning appearance. Place the vegetable mash mixture into a piping bag (or a resealable plastic bag with a 1-inch/ 2.5 cm corner cut off). Pipe desired design on top.

PASTA
AND OTHER
NOODLES

BROCCOLI AND KALE ASIAN NOODLE SALAD WITH MISO DRESSING

Making a quick, last-minute supper can be challenging, especially if you want it to be nutritious. This salad can be thrown together quickly with ingredients that are easy to find at the grocery store. You'll likely be able to purchase healthier ramen noodle options in the health food section of the store. Serve this salad alongside the Immune Boost Mason Jar Soup (page 73).

Serves 4 to 6 **DF**

BROCCOLI AND KALE ASIAN NOODLE SALAD

1 package (8 oz/230 g) broccoli-slaw mix

1 bunch kale, ribs removed and thinly sliced

1 cup (250 mL) toasted raw pistachios

1 cup (250 mL) sunflower seeds

1 bunch of green onion, thinly sliced

2 packages (each 3 oz/85 g) dried instant ramen noodles, any flavour, broken into smaller pieces; flavour packages discarded

MISO DRESSING

⅔ cup (150 mL) vegetable oil

⅓ cup (75 mL) white rice vinegar

¼ cup (60 mL) liquid honey

2 Tbsp (30 mL) soy sauce

2 tsp (10 mL) white miso

Place the broccoli-slaw mix, kale, pistachios, sunflower seeds and green onion in a large bowl and set aside.

In a small bowl, whisk the oil, vinegar, honey, soy sauce and miso together, and pour over the broccoli-kale mixture. Toss the dressing into the salad until evenly distributed. Toss the uncooked noodles in before serving.

GLUTEN-FREE OPTION Use *cooked* gluten-free noodles, replace the soy sauce with gluten-free tamari and the miso with gluten-free miso.

VEGAN OPTION Replace the honey with pure maple syrup.

TIP: If you want to replace the instant ramen with fresh or gluten-free varieties, cook 3.5 or 4 oz (100 or 115 g) of broken noodles until al dente or according to package instructions. Rinse with cold water and add to the salad.

GINGER LIME EDAMAME NOODLE BOWL

This fresh and vibrant Asian-inspired one-bowl meal makes a great dinner option, putting all your nutrients in one complete dish. Steaming hot edamame, sweet peppers and bean sprouts are served over sesame ginger soba noodles crowned with thinly sliced green onion. If you can't find soba, replace with black bean or edamame noodles. It's even tastier served with the Vegetable Nori Wraps with Orange Ginger Miso Dressing (page 37).

Serves 4 DF V

9 oz (255 g) 100% buckwheat
   soba noodles
2 Tbsp (30 mL) toasted sesame oil
1 Tbsp (15 mL) grapeseed oil
1 cup (250 mL) shelled edamame
1 tsp (5 mL) minced garlic
2 tsp (10 mL) grated fresh ginger
1 cup (250 mL) fresh bean sprouts,
   plus ½ cup (125 mL), to garnish
1 red bell pepper,
   thinly sliced into strips
1 yellow bell pepper,
   thinly sliced into strips
¼ tsp (1 mL) sea salt
3 Tbsp (45 mL) thinly sliced
   green onion
4 lime wedges
Soy sauce, for serving (optional)

Cook the noodles per package directions. Drain and gently toss with the sesame oil. Place in a bowl, cover and set aside.

Heat a large seasoned skillet or Dutch oven on low heat. Add the grapeseed oil, edamame, garlic and ginger. Cook for about 2 minutes or until the garlic and ginger are fragrant and the edamame is hot. Add the bean sprouts and peppers. Cook until the vegetables are crisp and hot. Season with salt.

Place the noodles in bowls and top each with the edamame mixture, bean sprouts, a sprinkle of green onion and a squeeze of lime. Sprinkle with soy sauce (if using). Serve.

GLUTEN-FREE OPTION Replace the soy sauce with gluten-free tamari.

TIP: If you don't require this dish to be gluten-free, you can use soba noodles that are not 100% buckwheat.

ASIAN PEANUT BLACK BEAN NOODLE SALAD

Black bean noodles are a great source of protein, fibre and iron. They also have half the carbohydrates of regular wheat pasta and are gluten-free. These noodles taste just as you'd expect pasta to taste and have a firm and slightly chewy texture. Mixed with crunchy cabbage, broccoli and a sweet peanutty sauce, this dish also makes for great leftovers or lunches the next day—even served cold. This salad is a pleasing addition to the Vegetable Nori Wraps with Orange Ginger Miso Dressing (page 37).

Serves 4 to 6

3½ oz (100 g) black bean noodles (about 2 cups/500 mL loose)

2½ cups (625 mL) thinly sliced purple cabbage

1½ cups (375 mL) bite-sized broccoli florets

1 sweet red pepper, cut into strips ½ inch (1 cm) wide and 1½ inches (4 cm) long

½ cup (125 mL) thinly sliced green onion (about 4)

2 Tbsp (30 mL) toasted sesame seeds

⅓ cup (75 mL) white rice vinegar

⅓ cup (75 mL) grapeseed oil

2 Tbsp (30 mL) pure maple syrup

1 Tbsp (15 mL) soy sauce

¼ to ½ tsp (1 to 2 mL) crushed hot pepper flakes

⅓ cup (75 mL) salted, shelled peanuts

Bring 5 cups (1.25 L) of water to a boil in a medium saucepan. Stir in the noodles and cook over medium heat for approximately 5 minutes or until tender. Drain and rinse with cold water. Place in a medium bowl. Add the cabbage, broccoli, red pepper, green onion and sesame seeds.

In a small bowl, whisk together the vinegar, oil, maple syrup, soy sauce and hot pepper flakes. Pour over and toss with the vegetable-noodle mixture. Sprinkle with peanuts before serving.

GLUTEN-FREE OPTION Replace the soy sauce with gluten-free tamari.

TIP: You may want to give the mixture a gentle toss to refresh if it has been sitting for any length of time.

SPAGHETTI SQUASH BUDDHA BOWL

This Buddha bowl is our version of an all-in-one dish filled with vegetable goodness to make you feel fabulous. The combination of spaghetti squash, carrots, mushrooms, tomatoes and beans, along with an herby sage pesto, will do just that.

Serves 4 GF

1 medium spaghetti squash, halved lengthwise, seeds removed

4 large carrots, washed, peeled, trimmed and chopped

2 cups (500 mL) button mushrooms

4 Roma tomatoes, chopped

8 pearl onions, trimmed, outer skins removed and chopped

1 can (19 oz/540 mL) kidney beans, rinsed and drained

SAGE PESTO

¼ cup (60 mL) fresh sage

¼ cup (60 mL) fresh parsley

1 tsp (5 mL) fresh thyme

¼ cup (60 mL) grated Parmesan cheese

¼ cup (60 mL) chopped walnuts

1 tsp (5 mL) minced garlic

¼ cup (60 mL) extra virgin olive oil

Pinch of sea salt

Preheat the oven to 400°F (200°C). Lightly spray with cooking oil or grease a 13- × 9-inch (3.5 L) baking dish and set aside.

Place the spaghetti squash halves flesh side down in the prepared pan. Add ½ cup (125 mL) of water and cover with foil. Bake for 20 to 25 minutes, and then add the carrots, mushrooms, tomatoes and onions to the baking squash. Cover again and bake for an additional 20 to 25 minutes or until squash flesh is soft and cooked through.

While the squash is baking, prepare the sage pesto. Place the sage, parsley, thyme, Parmesan cheese, walnuts, garlic, oil and salt in a blender or food processor and purée until smooth. Set aside.

Remove the baked squash and vegetables from the oven and set aside to cool slightly. Use a fork to scrape out the squash flesh. Rake your fork in the same direction as the strands of flesh to get a spaghetti-like texture.

Place equal amounts of the spaghetti squash in each serving dish, along with the roasted carrots, mushrooms, tomatoes, onions and the kidney beans. Dress each dish with a 1 or 2 tsp (5 or 10 mL) of the sage pesto.

CARROT RIBBONS WITH FETA AND PINE NUTS

Large noodle-like ribbons of fresh carrot are tossed with feta, pine nuts and fresh rosemary for a super simple, meatless, pasta-free noodle dish. Delicious couldn't be any simpler! Using a variety of colourful rainbow carrots will make this salad look even more unbelievable. Build a full meal and serve these veggie-noodles alongside a thick slab of the Meatless Meatloaf (page 162).

Serves 4 as a side or 2 as a main **GF**

¼ cup (60 mL) pine nuts
6 large carrots, peeled
¼ cup (60 mL) crumbled
   feta cheese
1 tsp (5 mL) chopped
   fresh rosemary

Heat a large skillet on medium heat. Place the pine nuts in the pan and stir frequently for a few minutes or until fragrant and lightly toasted. Remove the nuts from the pan and set aside in a small bowl.

Use a handheld cheese slicer to slice the carrots into large, flat strips. The strips should be the width of the carrots, approximately 1 to 1½ inches (2.5 to 4 cm). Place the strips in a steamer or saucepan of water, and gently steam or cook for 3 to 4 minutes or until just tender. Remove the strips from the steamer, place in a medium-large serving bowl and toss with the feta cheese, toasted pine nuts and rosemary. Serve.

DAIRY-FREE OPTION Replace the feta cheese with soy, nut, seed or other dairy-free cheese.

VEGAN OPTION Replace the feta cheese with soy, nut, seed or other vegan cheese.

RAW OPTION Replace the toasted pine nuts with untoasted, don't steam the carrots and use raw nut or seed cheese.

> TIP: Don't have a handheld cheese slicer? Use a wide vegetable peeler to slice large, flat strips of carrot.

SOBA NOODLES WITH RAPINI AND SNOW PEAS

Soba noodles are traditionally buckwheat noodles. Unfortunately, you will find many brands that have little to no buckwheat in them at all—so read the package ingredients carefully and pick one with buckwheat for better nutrition. In this recipe, soba noodles are cooked gently, then sautéed with snow peas and rapini for a crunchy, vegetable-noodle dish.

Serves 2

TAHINI DRESSING
2 Tbsp (30 mL) tahini
2 Tbsp (30 mL) sesame oil
2 Tbsp (30 mL) water
1 Tbsp (15 mL) soy sauce
½ Tbsp (7 mL) mirin, sweet marsala
    or dry sherry
1 Tbsp (15 mL) fresh lemon juice
½ tsp (2 mL) minced fresh ginger
½ tsp (2 mL) minced garlic

3½ oz (100 g) 100% buckwheat
    soba noodles
1 to 2 Tbsp (15 to 30 mL) sesame oil
    or grapeseed oil
1 bunch fresh rapini, washed
    and trimmed
1 cup (250 mL) snow peas
1 cup (250 mL) canned water
    chestnuts, drained
Sea salt and ground black pepper,
    to taste

Combine the tahini, 2 Tbsp (30 mL) of sesame oil, water, soy sauce, mirin, lemon juice, ginger and garlic in a small jar, or whisk in a small bowl and set aside.

Bring a medium saucepan of water to a boil. Add the noodles and cook, uncovered, for 5 to 7 minutes or until the pasta is tender or according to package instructions. Drain and toss with a portion of the dressing, to taste, and set aside.

Place 1 to 2 Tbsp (15 to 30 mL) of sesame oil in a large saucepan over medium-low heat. Sauté the rapini for 3 to 5 minutes, just to slightly wilt it, then add the snow peas and water chestnuts and continue to cook for 1 to 2 minutes, until warm. Remove from the heat. Season with salt and pepper. Place a serving of noodles on each plate, topped with the vegetable mixture. Add more dressing as desired.

GLUTEN-FREE OPTION Replace the soy sauce with gluten-free tamari.

TIP: If you don't require this dish to be gluten-free, you can use soba noodles that are not 100% buckwheat.

ASPARAGUS AND PORCINI LO MEIN

This is a full and satisfying meal—no sides required! Whole-grain noodles are combined with asparagus and the woodsy, earthy flavour of porcini mushrooms to make a dish that has plenty of bite. The bold, robust flavour and meaty texture of porcini mushrooms make them a great foundation in any meatless dish.

Serves 4

8 oz (230 g) whole wheat spaghettini pasta

1 to 2 Tbsp (15 to 30 mL) grapeseed oil, divided

2 Tbsp (30 mL) finely chopped shallots

2/3 cup (150 mL) chopped porcini mushrooms (see Tip)

2 tsp (10 mL) minced garlic

1 cup (250 mL) Simple Vegetable Broth (page 62) or low-sodium, store-bought vegetable broth

2 cups (500 mL) asparagus, tough ends trimmed

1 tsp (5 mL) cornstarch

1½ tsp (7 mL) fresh lemon juice

1½ tsp (7 mL) chopped fresh thyme

¼ tsp (1 mL) sea salt

Bring a large saucepan of water to a boil. Add the spaghettini and cook, uncovered, for 5 to 7 minutes or until the pasta is tender or according to package instructions. Drain and toss with 1 tsp (5 mL) of oil, place in a large bowl and set aside.

Combine the remaining oil and the shallots in a large saucepan over medium heat. Sauté for 3 to 5 minutes or until soft and beginning to brown. Add the mushrooms and garlic, and continue to cook for another 3 to 5 minutes or until the mushrooms are almost cooked. Add the broth and asparagus and bring to a boil. Cook for 3 to 5 minutes or until the asparagus is tender. Reduce the heat and add the cornstarch. Simmer until the mixture slightly thickens. Remove from the heat and add the lemon juice and thyme. Add the pasta and toss to combine. Season with the salt and serve.

GLUTEN-FREE OPTION Replace the whole wheat spaghettini with gluten-free spaghettini or spaghetti.

> TIP: Dried or fresh mushrooms? If you can't find fresh porcini mushrooms, dried are just as good. For this recipe, simply soak 1 oz (30 g) of dried porcini mushrooms in a bowl of water for 30 minutes. The mushrooms will be rehydrated, full of flavour and ready to use.

BAKED EGGPLANT PARMESAN
OVER HOMEMADE SOURDOUGH NOODLES

Crispy baked eggplant Parmesan is topped with hot tomato sauce and fresh basil, and served over tender handmade sourdough noodles. This is a healthier version of the classic, but still maintains a delightful fried flavour—without being fried! Fermented sourdough starter used in the noodles benefits digestion and healthy gut bacteria. Sourdough noodles are incredibly addictive, so don't wait to make your Sourdough Starter (page 205)!

Serves 4 to 6

SOURDOUGH NOODLES
1½ cups (375 mL) all-purpose flour
¼ tsp (1 mL) sea salt
1 large egg
2 egg yolks
½ cup (125 mL) Sourdough Starter
 (page 205)

BAKED EGGPLANT PARMESAN
1 tsp (5 mL) chopped fresh thyme
1 Tbsp (15 mL) salted butter, melted
1½ cups (375 mL) fine dry
 breadcrumbs
½ cup (125 mL) all-purpose or rice
 flour
2 large eggs, beaten
2 small (1 lb/450 g) eggplants, cut
 into slices ¼ inch (5 mm) thick
1½ cups (375 mL) marinara sauce
1 cup (250 mL) shredded mozzarella
 cheese
¼ cup (60 mL) grated Parmesan
 cheese
2 Tbsp (30 mL) fresh basil,
 chiffonade (see Tip on page 102)

Whisk the flour and salt together in a medium bowl. Form a well in the flour. Whisk the egg, yolks and sourdough starter together in a small bowl until fully mixed. Pour into the well of flour. Use clean hands to knead dough. The dough should be sticky enough to cling to the hands but release and leave little or none remaining. Knead the dough for 2 minutes, then wrap in plastic wrap and refrigerate for 3 hours to allow the flour to hydrate and the dough to become tender.

Remove the dough from the refrigerator and set aside the plastic wrap. Cut in half and flatten with your hands. Flour your rolling surface and roll out the dough until it is ¼ inch (5 mm) thick. Using a pizza cutter and ruler, cut into noodles ¼ inch (5 mm) wide. Flour your hands and separate the noodles. Hang them over the edge of a large bowl and set aside.

Meanwhile, preheat the oven to 425°F (220°C) and line a large baking sheet with parchment paper or a silicone mat. In a medium bowl, work the thyme and melted butter evenly into the breadcrumbs with your hands. Set up three shallow bowls for breading the eggplant: one with the flour, one with the beaten eggs and one with the breadcrumb mixture. Start to bread the eggplant by using your left hand to coat the eggplant in flour, then coat it in the beaten egg. Use your right hand to transfer it to the breadcrumb bowl and coat each piece completely. Transfer to the baking sheet and continue breading the remainder of the eggplant slices. Place the baking sheet in the oven and bake for 10 minutes or until the breaded eggplant is golden brown. Remove from the oven and set aside.

...continued

Preheat the oven to broil. Place the marinara sauce in a small saucepan and heat over medium-low until heated throughout. With the eggplant still on the baking sheet, spoon 1 Tbsp (15 mL) of sauce over each slice of baked eggplant. Top with mozzarella cheese and a pinch or two of Parmesan cheese. Place under the broiler for about 3 minutes or until the tops are golden brown and bubbling. Remove from the oven and set aside.

In a large stockpot, bring 6 quarts (6 L) of water to a rolling boil. Place the sourdough pasta into the water, and cook for 1 to 2 minutes or until hot and tender. Do not overcook. Drain the water and toss the noodles with a touch of oil.

Place a serving of pasta on each plate. Top with the remainder of the hot marinara sauce, the eggplant Parmesan pieces and a pinch of fresh basil. Serve immediately.

BROKEN LASAGNA
WITH POBLANO PEPPERS AND MUSHROOMS

Easier than the traditional baked version, a broken lasagna is the lasagna-lover's quick fix! This one has a veggie tomato sauce perked up with the natural smoky flavour of poblano peppers and earthy, chunky portobello mushrooms.

Serves 4

1 Tbsp (15 mL) grapeseed oil
1 cup (250 mL) chopped
    white onion
2 cups (500 mL) chopped
    portobello mushrooms
1 cup (250 mL) chopped zucchini
2 tsp (10 mL) minced garlic
1 cup (250 mL) chopped and
    seeded poblano peppers
2 cups (500 mL) tomato sauce
2 tsp (10 mL) organic cane sugar or
    white sugar
½ tsp (2 mL) ground cumin
½ tsp (2 mL) ground coriander
½ tsp (2 mL) ground chili powder
½ tsp (2 mL) smoked paprika
½ tsp (2 mL) dried marjoram
¼ tsp (1 mL) red pepper flakes
1 Tbsp (15 mL) fresh lime juice
Pinch of cayenne pepper
Sea salt and ground black pepper,
    to taste
1 cup (250 mL) shredded
    mozzarella cheese
½ cup (125 mL) dry or creamed
    cottage cheese
¼ cup (60 mL) chopped
    fresh cilantro
¼ cup (60 mL) chopped
    fresh parsley
8 oz (230 g) lasagna noodles,
    broken into bite-sized pieces
2 cups (500 mL) chopped
    Swiss chard

Heat the oil in a large saucepan over medium heat, and sauté the onion until soft and translucent, about 4 to 5 minutes. Add the mushrooms, zucchini, garlic and peppers, and continue to cook for another 3 to 5 minutes, until the mushrooms are almost cooked. Add the tomato sauce and reduce to a simmer. Add the sugar, cumin, coriander, chili powder, paprika, marjoram, red pepper flakes, lime juice, cayenne, salt and pepper. Simmer for 10 to 12 minutes or until the mixture slightly thickens. Remove from the heat. Set aside.

Combine the mozzarella cheese, cottage cheese, cilantro and parsley in a medium bowl, and mix together. Set aside.

Bring a large saucepan of water to a boil. Place the lasagna noodles in the water, stirring occasionally for 12 to 14 minutes or until tender but firm or according to package instructions. Add the chard during the last minute of cooking. Drain the pasta and chard.

Toss the pasta, chard and sauce together in the saucepan. Divide the mixture into separate serving bowls and sprinkle each with cheese mixture.

GLUTEN-FREE OPTION Replace the lasagna noodles with gluten-free noodles.

> TIP: If you can't find poblano peppers, use bell peppers and simply add ¼ tsp (1 mL) of ancho chili powder to the sauce.

ZUCCHINI-TOMATO PASTA
WITH GARLIC THYME CASHEW CREAM

You may find it hard to cook with anything but wheat pasta, until you make quick-cooking zucchini noodles! The flavour in this dish will have family and guests devouring it like a pack of wolves. Quickly preparing the spiralized zucchini and cashew cream the night before will reduce the cooking time even further.

Serves 4 to 6 **DF** **GF** **V**

GARLIC THYME CASHEW CREAM
1 cup (250 mL) toasted,
    unsalted cashews
1¾ cups plus 1 Tbsp (440 mL) water,
    divided
1 tsp (5 mL) minced garlic
1 tsp (5 mL) chopped fresh thyme
¼ tsp (1 mL) sea salt
Pinch of freshly ground pepper

1 Tbsp (15 mL) grapeseed oil
1 Tbsp (15 mL) water
3 small to medium (1½ lbs/680 g)
    zucchini, spiralized
½ pint grape tomatoes, halved
1 lemon, zested
¼ to ⅓ cup (60 to 75 mL) grated
    Parmesan cheese (optional)

Place the cashews in a bowl and cover with 1 cup (250 mL) of water. Let soak for 2 hours or refrigerate overnight. Drain the cashews and rinse.

Heat a large saucepan or Dutch oven over medium-low heat. Add the oil, 1 Tbsp (15 mL) of water, zucchini and tomatoes. Cover and let cook for about 4 minutes. Remove the lid and let the liquid reduce. Cook until the vegetables are tender-crisp and not mushy.

Add the soaked cashews and ½ cup (125 mL) of water to a blender and purée until smooth. Place the cashew cream in a medium saucepan and heat on medium-low. Stir in the garlic and thyme. Whisk in the remaining ¼ cup (60 mL) of water to make the sauce the consistency of traditional Alfredo or cream sauce. When heated, season with the salt and pepper.

Plate the hot pasta and top with the sauce and a touch of lemon zest. Sprinkle with Parmesan cheese (if using). Skip the Parmesan cheese if you require it to be dairy-free or vegan.

> TIP: Spiralizers are a handy kitchen tool. Small handheld spiralizers are inexpensive and widely available, or you can opt for a larger, counter-top model. If you don't have a spiralizer, use a vegetable peeler to cut thin ribbons of zucchini instead.

BUTTERNUT SQUASH AND BLACK KALE RAVIOLI TOSS WITH PARMESAN CHEESE

Black kale, also known as Tuscan kale, is the superstar of Italian dishes with its mild flavour and huge nutritional value. The health benefits are extensive, with a single serving providing 100 percent of the daily value of vitamins A and K, as well as 80 percent of vitamin C. Tender butternut squash and creamy cheese ravioli balance the earthiness of the kale. Top it with fresh grated Parmesan cheese, and you've got a superstar meal. Add a decadent touch and serve this dish with the Roasted Cauliflower Soup with Tarragon Brown Butter (page 69).

Serves 4 to 6

3 cups (750 mL) cheese ravioli
3 Tbsp (45 mL) Clarified Butter (page 194)
½ cup (125 mL) onion, cut into slices ½ inch (1 cm) thick
3½ cups (875 mL) diced butternut squash
3½ cups (875 mL) chopped black kale, ribs removed
1 clove garlic, minced
Pinch of sea salt
⅓ cup (75 mL) grated Parmesan cheese
Raw pepitas, to garnish (optional)

In a large saucepan, bring 10 cups (2.5 L) of water to a boil. Add the ravioli and cook until al dente or according to package instructions. Rinse with cold water, cover and set aside.

Preheat the same large saucepan on medium-low heat. Add the Clarified Butter and onion. Cover and cook for about 3 minutes. Place the squash on top, cover and cook for 5 more minutes. Stir in the kale, garlic and salt. Cover and cook for another 10 minutes or until the squash and kale are tender but not mushy. Gently stir in the ravioli and heat through. Top with Parmesan cheese and garnish with pepitas (if using).

SPINACH AND CHEESE BAKED ZUCCHINI CANNELLONI

This cannelloni recipe has the wow-factor trifecta! Nutrition, beauty and amazing flavour without pasta! Neatly wrapped zucchini packets of cottage cheese and spinach are loaded with fresh herbs and baked in a light tomato sauce, sprinkled with Parmesan cheese. This dish can even be made the night before, stored in the refrigerator and baked the next day. Partner it up with the Tossed Baby Arugula and Zucchini Salad (page 90).

Serves 2 to 4 GF

1 Tbsp (15 mL) grapeseed oil
¼ cup (60 mL) chopped onion
1 tsp (5 mL) minced garlic
1 cup (250 mL) tomato sauce
1 tsp (5 mL) organic cane sugar
　or white sugar
1¼ cups (300 mL) pressed cottage
　cheese
1 large egg
1 cup (250 mL) chopped spinach
3 Tbsp (45 mL) chopped
　fresh basil
2 Tbsp (30 mL) chopped
　fresh parsley
2 to 3 large zucchini, peeled and
　sliced into 30 strips approximately
　1½ to 2 inches (4 to 5 cm) wide
　and 5 to 7 inches (12.5 to 17.5 cm)
　long
⅓ cup (75 mL) grated
　Parmesan cheese
Basil leaves, to garnish (optional)

Preheat the oven to 350°F (180°C). Line a 13- × 9-inch (3.5 L) baking dish with parchment paper and set aside.

Combine the oil, onion and garlic in a medium saucepan over medium heat. Sauté until the onion is soft and the edges are beginning to brown, 3 to 5 minutes. Reduce to a simmer, add the tomato sauce and sugar, and continue to cook for 2 to 3 minutes or until sauce is heated through. Spread half of the sauce in the bottom of the prepared pan and set the remainder aside.

Mix the cottage cheese and egg in a medium bowl. Add the spinach, basil and parsley. Set aside.

Place two strips of zucchini perpendicular to each other and overlapping (like a plus sign) on a clean, dry workspace, countertop or cutting board. Place 1 Tbsp (15 mL) of cottage cheese mixture in centre of the zucchini, where the two strips intersect. Fold over each of the four ends of the strips to create a small square packet. Place the packet on top of the sauce in the prepared baking dish. Continue to create packets with the zucchini and cottage cheese mixture until you have 15 packets in the sauce-lined baking dish.

Spread remaining sauce on top of zucchini packets. Sprinkle the top with Parmesan cheese. Bake in the oven for 25 to 30 minutes or until the edges are bubbling and golden. Garnish with basil (if using).

> TIP: We prefer to cut large, flat zucchini strips with a handheld cheese slicer or very carefully use a mandoline.

ROASTED RED PEPPER AND PUMPKIN LASAGNA

The delicious flavours of autumn converge into a nutritional powerhouse! This vegetable-packed recipe boasts herbed spinach, mushrooms and zesty roasted red pepper tomato sauce in a cheesy and rich lasagna with pumpkin ricotta filling. Salivating yet? Serve it with the Raw Shaved Asparagus Salad with Dulse and Parmesan (page 95).

Serves 6 to 8

2 cups (500 mL) ricotta cheese

1 can (14 oz/398 mL) pure pumpkin purée

2 large eggs

1 tsp (5 mL) minced garlic

½ tsp (2 mL) sea salt

¼ tsp (1 mL) ground black pepper

1 Tbsp (15 mL) grapeseed oil or vegetable oil

1 package (12 oz/300 g) frozen chopped spinach, thawed and squeezed out

1 package (1 lb/450 g) sliced white mushrooms

1 cup (250 mL) chopped yellow onion

1½ tsp (7 mL) herbs de Provence

2 roasted red peppers, seeds and stem removed (see page 199)

1 cup (250 mL) tomato sauce

1 package (12 oz/350 g) fresh lasagna sheets or no-boil lasagna noodles

2 cups (500 mL) shredded mozzarella cheese

½ cup (125 mL) grated Parmesan cheese

2 tsp (10 mL) chopped fresh parsley (optional)

Mix together the ricotta cheese, pumpkin, eggs, garlic, salt and pepper in a medium bowl. Set aside.

Heat a large skillet over medium-low heat. Combine the oil, spinach, mushrooms, onion and herbs de Provence in the skillet, and cook until the onion is tender, about 7 to 10 minutes. Set aside.

Purée the roasted red peppers and tomato sauce in a blender until smooth.

Preheat the oven to 350°F (180°C). Assemble the lasagna by placing 2 Tbsp (30 mL) of water in the bottom of a 13- × 9-inch (3.5 L) baking dish. Place a single layer of noodles in the bottom. Cut or break noodles where necessary. Spread half of the spinach mushroom mixture over the noodles. Spread half of the ricotta mixture next, then the roasted red pepper sauce. Repeat the layers once more. Top with the last layer of lasagna sheets and cover with the mozzarella and Parmesan cheeses.

Cover with oiled foil (the side next to the cheese) and bake for 45 minutes. Remove the foil and bake for an additional 10 minutes or until the cheese is bubbling and golden. Remove from the oven and let rest before serving. Sprinkle with a touch of chopped parsley (if using).

GLUTEN-FREE OPTION Use al dente or slightly under-cooked gluten-free lasagna noodles.

HOMEMADE STAPLES

BUTTER

Making your own creamy butter is so much easier than you'd think, and all you need is heavy cream or whipping cream. We prefer organic cream and find that it provides the best flavour. Unsalted or salted, it's up to you. You'll simply need a few tools including a stand mixer, cheesecloth, medium bowl, spatula and a fine mesh strainer.

Makes 2 cups (500 mL) **GF**

4 cups (1 L) 35% whipping cream
3 to 5 cups (750 mL to 1.25 L)
  ice cold water
Sea salt, to taste

Place the cream in the bowl of the stand mixer and whip on medium speed until stiff peaks form. Continue whipping until the water starts to separate from the milk solids. Continue mixing on medium-low until the milk solids have separated and become thick.

Place a few layers of cheesecloth in a strainer and set over a medium-sized bowl. Pour the mixing bowl contents into the strainer to catch the solids. Drain off the liquid and store for later use. (This is a light buttermilk that you can use in other recipes, up until the best before date on the container of cream used.)

Place the butter solids back in the mixing bowl. Add 1 cup (250 mL) of ice water to the butter, and using a spatula or clean hands, push out any air and buttermilk trapped within the solids. The water will become cloudy. Discard the water and repeat this washing process with another 1 cup (250 mL) of ice water. Repeat until the water stays clear. Discard the final rinse water and add salt to the butter if desired.

Press into shallow mason jars or a parchment-lined loaf pan. Refrigerate and cut into usable pieces. Rewrap the smaller pieces with parchment paper and place in a resealable bag for freezing. Use as desired. This butter will keep for up to 6 months in the refrigerator.

> TIP: Why rinse the solids? The removal of the buttermilk will greatly extend the shelf life of the butter. Do it unless you are going to use the butter right away or within 2 days.

CLARIFIED BUTTER

Clarified butter retains a distinctive rich flavour, but unlike traditional butter, it contains no milk solids, water and salt. Clarifying the butter increases the smoke point, which makes it a great option for cooking at higher temperatures. It will keep for 6 months or more in the refrigerator. It may become solid at cooler temperatures but will liquefy when warm. Make sure to have some cheesecloth and a fine mesh strainer on hand for this recipe.

Makes 1 cup (250 mL) **GF**

1 lb (450 g) unsalted butter

In a heavy-bottomed saucepan, slowly melt the butter. Once completely melted, remove from the heat. Use a large spoon to skim the milk solids, water and salt from the top and store for later use (up until the best before date of the butter used).

Place a few layers of cheesecloth in a fine strainer over a medium bowl. Pour the melted butter into the strainer. Remove the cheesecloth and strainer. Pour the clarified butter into one or two mason jars and refrigerate for up to 6 months.

> TIP: You can use the leftover milk solids in other recipes, such as melting on top of steamed vegetables or stirring into hot pasta.

NATURAL PLAIN YOGURT

Yogurt can be made with a "starter" culture and a yogurt maker if you choose, but it's just as easy to make at home with whole milk and any quality yogurt with active bacterial cultures, even store-bought. You have the option to make it a more traditional, lighter consistency or a thick Greek-style yogurt. Either way is simple and delicious! The tools you'll need are a slow cooker, instant-read thermometer, cheesecloth and a fine mesh strainer.

Makes 2 cups (500 mL)

4 cups (1 L) whole milk (3.25% milk fat)

½ cup (125 mL) plain yogurt, unsweetened (with active bacterial cultures in the ingredients list)

Place the milk in the slow cooker or Dutch oven and heat to 180°F (85°C). In the slow cooker, it can take as long as 1½ hours; in a Dutch oven, heat for 10 minutes over medium-low heat. Turn off the slow cooker or remove the Dutch oven from the heat and allow the milk to cool to 110°F to 115°F (44°C to 46°C), about 20 to 30 minutes.

Gently stir in the yogurt, lightly whisking it into the milk. Cover with the lid and wrap the unplugged slow cooker or the Dutch oven in a towel and leave it on the counter for about 10 hours. Alternatively, you can place the slow cooker insert or Dutch oven in the oven with the light on. After 10 hours, remove the lid. The yogurt will have developed and thickened.

Place a fine mesh strainer over a medium metal or glass bowl. Line the strainer with a few layers of cheesecloth. Pour the yogurt into the cheesecloth and let it sit in the refrigerator for a few hours to drain off the liquid, or whey. If you prefer a thicker yogurt, let it drain twice as long. If you want to make it into yogurt cheese (a great store-bought cream cheese substitute), refrigerate it overnight in the strainer. Use a spatula to remove the yogurt from the cloth. Place in desired storage container in the refrigerator for up to 2 weeks.

> TIP: The drained off whey is healthy and can be used in smoothies. It is high in protein and low in lactose and contains all nine essential amino acids.

TOMATO KETCHUP

Store-bought ketchup can be laden with sugar and sodium, so we like to make a batch of our own to control the amount we consume. Not only is this homemade condiment healthier, but it can easily be made with familiar ingredients in a slow cooker or by simmering on the stove.

Makes 1 cup (250 mL) DF GF V

1 can (28 oz/796 mL) puréed
    tomatoes
⅓ cup (75 mL) brown sugar or
    organic cane sugar
⅓ cup (75 mL) apple cider vinegar
¼ cup (60 mL) minced
    yellow onion
2 tsp (10 mL) tomato paste
1 clove garlic, minced
¾ tsp (3 mL) sea salt
Pinch of celery salt
Pinch of dry mustard
Pinch of ground black pepper
Pinch of paprika

Place the tomatoes, sugar, vinegar, onion, tomato paste, garlic, salt, celery salt, mustard, pepper and paprika into a slow cooker. Cook on high for 8 to 10 hours, stirring occasionally.

Place a couple of layers of cheesecloth in a fine mesh strainer over a medium-sized bowl. Pour the ketchup into the cheesecloth and strain off the solids, such as garlic bits and tomato seeds, which can then be discarded. Press through the strainer with the back of a spoon, if required.

Place the ketchup in a small saucepan and bring to a simmer until thickened to the desired consistency. Add a touch of water if necessary. Season again with additional salt if desired.

Store in a mason jar in the refrigerator for up to 6 weeks. The ketchup can be used immediately after making, but the flavours will improve even more if left overnight.

YELLOW MUSTARD

Both mustard seeds and turmeric are thought to have anti-inflammatory properties, as they're rich in selenium and magnesium. Not only is it nutritionally beneficial, but it takes very little time to prepare homemade mustard and it lasts in the refrigerator for 4 months or longer. Enhance your meals with the flavour of homemade mustard!

Makes 1 cup (250 mL)

⅓ cup (75 mL) water
¼ cup (60 mL) white wine vinegar
⅓ cup (75 mL) yellow mustard seeds
½ tsp (2 mL) ground turmeric
½ tsp (2 mL) sea salt
Pinch of paprika

Bring the water and vinegar to a boil. Add the mustard seeds and reduce to a simmer for 1 minute. Stir in the turmeric, salt and paprika. Remove from the heat and let sit, covered, for at least 1 hour to fully release the flavours.

Purée with an immersion blender or in a blender until smooth. Season again with additional salt, or thin with a touch of water if desired. Refrigerate overnight for best flavour. Store in the refrigerator in a mason jar for 4 months or longer.

CREAMY MAYONNAISE

Delicious, freshly made mayonnaise is beyond compare! Make it easily with basic whole ingredients—and that means there are no additives.

Makes 1½ cups (375 mL) DF GF R

2 cold large egg yolks
2 tsp (10 mL) apple cider vinegar
1 to 2 tsp (5 to 10 mL) fresh lemon
   juice
¼ tsp (1 mL) Dijon mustard
¼ tsp (1 mL) sea salt
¾ cup (175 mL) grapeseed oil,
   room temperature

Place the egg yolks, vinegar, lemon juice, Dijon and salt in a medium bowl or stand mixer. Beat on medium speed until the mixture is yellow and blended. Continue beating and pour a very slow steady stream of oil into the egg mixture. The eggs and oil should start to emulsify and turn into creamy thick mayonnaise. Store in a glass jar in the refrigerator for up to 10 days.

> TIP: Raw egg is not recommended for pregnant women, seniors, infants or anyone with a compromised immune system because of salmonella bacteria. If needed, replace raw egg with pasteurized eggs instead. Pasteurized eggs have been thoroughly cleaned with heat so no bacteria remains.

BLUE CHEESE DIP

This is the real McCoy of blue cheese dips. Store-bought dressings can't compete with the flavour of this homemade favourite. Serve with vegetables, with Crispy Buffalo Cauliflower Bites (page 40) or as a replacement dressing in the Lazy Layered Salad (page 102). If you want to make a thinner version for a salad dressing, use kefir or buttermilk, and if you want a thicker dip, use sour cream.

Makes 1 cup (250 mL)

½ cup (125 mL) kefir, buttermilk or sour cream
½ cup (125 mL) Creamy Mayonnaise (page 197) or store-bought
2 oz (55 g) blue cheese, crumbled
½ tsp (2 mL) minced garlic or ¼ tsp (1 mL) garlic powder
½ tsp (2 mL) Worcestershire sauce (vegan) (optional)
¼ tsp (1 mL) sea salt
Pinch of ground black pepper

In a medium bowl, combine the kefir, mayonnaise, blue cheese, garlic, Worcestershire (if using), salt and pepper. Whisk together until blended but with some cheese crumbles remaining. Use immediately or let sit overnight for improved flavour.

GLUTEN-FREE OPTION Use gluten-free Worcestershire sauce or skip it completely if you don't have any.

MISO MUSHROOM GRAVY

Made in minutes, this simple gravy has a rich, savoury flavour from the earthy mushroom broth, but you can use vegetable broth if you prefer. Either will provide a true gravy flavour to complement meatless dishes. Try this gravy on our tasty Meatless Meatloaf (page 162).

Makes approximately 2 cups (500 mL) DF V

1½ cups (375 mL) Simple Mushroom Broth (page 61)
2 tsp (10 mL) red miso
3 Tbsp (45 mL) all-purpose flour
¼ tsp (1 mL) ground black pepper
Sea salt, to taste (optional)

Place the broth in a medium saucepan over medium-high heat. Whisk the miso into the hot broth. When the miso is completely incorporated, slowly whisk in the flour, constantly stirring to avoid lumps. Add more broth or water to adjust desired thickness. Add pepper and salt (if using), to taste. Store in the refrigerator for up to 4 days for optimal freshness.

ROASTED BELL PEPPERS

Roasting adds a whole new realm of flavour to almost any vegetable, and peppers are definitely one of them. Buying prepared roasted peppers from the store might save time, but they can be expensive. You can use these in many delicious dishes, including sandwiches, soups, salads, sauces and dips. They freeze beautifully, so if you have any extras, just toss them in your freezer. All you need for this is your oven or barbecue, some aluminum foil and a brown paper bag.

Makes approximately 2 cups (500 mL)

4 bell peppers, halved lengthwise and seeded

Preheat the oven to broil. Line a baking sheet with aluminum foil and place the peppers cut side down. Bake for 12 to 15 minutes on each side. The peppers will become blackened, collapsed and wrinkly. If they still look firm, place them back in the oven for another 15 minutes.

Place the roasted peppers in a paper bag, fold the top closed and place on a large plate. (Another option is to put them in a bowl and cover with plastic wrap.) Let them rest for 20 to 30 minutes. The skin and stem can be removed easily at this point. Cool and use as desired. Refrigerate for up to 3 days or freeze for up to 1 month.

> TIP: Instead of using your oven broiler (which requires the use of an overhead fan), use an outdoor barbecue to char the peppers skin side down. This process is quicker, so check and turn the peppers every 5 minutes.

SPICED CAULIFLOWER AND CARROT REFRIGERATOR PICKLES

Slightly spiced and seasoned cauliflower and carrots are ideal served as a side dish, appetizer, condiment or tapas dish.

Makes 4 cups (1 L)   V

4 cloves garlic, peeled
   and smashed
2½ cups (625 mL) bite-sized
   cauliflower pieces
¾ cup (175 mL) sweet carrot sticks
¼ cup (60 mL) thinly sliced onion
1 hot pepper, such as scotch
   bonnet, jalapeño or Thai red chili
   pepper (optional)
1½ cups (375 mL) distilled water
1½ cups (375 mL) apple cider
   vinegar
3 Tbsp (45 mL) white sugar or
   organic cane sugar
3 Tbsp (45 mL) sea salt
½ tsp (2 mL) mustard seeds

Place the garlic in the bottom of a sterilized 4-cup (1 L) mason jar. Add the cauliflower, carrots, onion and hot pepper (if using) to the jar until 1 inch (2.5 cm) of space remains at the top. Set aside.

Bring the water, vinegar, sugar, salt and mustard seeds to a boil in a medium saucepan. Reduce to a simmer and cook for 5 minutes or until the salt and sugar have dissolved. Pour the hot mixture over the vegetables until 1 inch (2.5 cm) of space remains at the top of the jar. Lightly secure the lid and set aside to cool on the counter. Once cooled, tighten the lid and place in the refrigerator for a minimum of 1 week for best results. Store in the refrigerator for up to 2 months.

REFRIGERATOR DILL PICKLES

This is an easy recipe for a classic pickle made in a small batch, saving you from having to make several jars at once! Try them along with the Caramelized Onion with Gruyère and Sauerkraut on Dark Rye (page 132).

Makes 4 cups (1 L) **DF** **GF** **V**

2 cloves garlic, peeled
   and smashed
2 cups (500 mL) cucumber spears or
   pickling cucumbers, thoroughly
   washed and dried
2 large sprigs of dill
1⅓ cups (325 mL) distilled water
⅔ cup (150 mL) gluten-free
   white vinegar
2 Tbsp (30 mL) sea salt

Place the garlic in the bottom of a sterilized 4-cup (1 L) mason jar. Place the cucumber spears or pickling cucumbers in the jar, leaving ¾ inch (2 cm) of space at the top, followed by the dill. Set aside.

Bring the water, vinegar and salt to a boil. Reduce to a simmer and cook until the salt has dissolved, about 5 minutes. Pour the hot mixture over the cucumbers until ¾ inch (2 cm) of space remains at the top of the jar. Lightly secure the lid and allow the jar to cool on the counter. Once cooled, tighten the lid and place in the refrigerator for a minimum of 1 week for best results. Store in the refrigerator for up to 2 months.

PORTOBELLO BACON

Don't be fooled by the notion that eating meatless means doing without those addictive, full-flavour comfort foods, like bacon. This portobello bacon will take you to your happy place and satisfy that craving. Salty and savoury, with a touch of fat and a chewy texture, serve this dish anywhere you would normally serve real bacon.

Serves 1

2 tsp (10 mL) salted butter
1 portobello mushroom, cut into
   slices ¼ inch (5 mm) thick
1 Tbsp (15 mL) soy sauce
Pinch of smoked paprika

Heat a wide-bottomed saucepan over medium heat. Melt the butter and add the portobello slices. Cook, covered, until the mushrooms start to sweat and release moisture.

Remove the lid and stir in the soy sauce and paprika. Gently stir until each mushroom piece has been coated. Ensure each mushroom slice is flat on the bottom of the saucepan.

Flip when the mushrooms get slightly crispy on one side. Cook the other side until slightly crispy.

Remove from the heat and serve immediately if using like real bacon, or cool slightly before chopping into bacon bits. It is best when used immediately or within 4 days. Store in the refrigerator in a resealable container.

GLUTEN-FREE OPTION Replace the soy sauce with gluten-free tamari.

DULSE BACON BITS

When salty, earthy dulse leaves are sautéed with oil and a squeeze of lemon, they become a zesty, briny topping that resembles savoury bacon bits. Make a large batch and keep on hand to use on all kinds of savoury salads, casseroles and soups.

Makes ⅓ cup (75 mL)

½ cup (125 mL) dulse leaves,
   washed and rehydrated in water
1 to 2 Tbsp (15 to 30 mL)
   grapeseed oil
½ tsp (2 mL) fresh lemon juice

Rinse the dulse thoroughly so that no small shells or stones remain in the leaves. Place the oil in a large skillet over medium-low heat and sauté the dulse until it is dry and resembles fine crumbs. If the skillet dries, add small amounts of oil until the dulse is cooked to the desired texture. It should look similar to cooked ground beef.

Remove the pan from heat. Sprinkle with lemon juice and stir. Cool slightly. Serve on salads and in dishes you would garnish with bacon bits. It will keep fresh in a sealed container in the refrigerator for up to 1 week.

> TIP: Why eat dulse? Not only is it fibre and protein rich, but dulse is high in vitamins A, C, E, B6, B12. It's also a great source of calcium, magnesium and iodine, a mineral we are often deficient in but that is an important part of overall health.

CRISP AND SMOKY CROUTONS

A perfect complement to vegetarian dishes, crispy croutons add salty and smoky flavour. Use these on top of a casserole or baked dish, or you might even enjoy them as a snack all on their own. Croutons make a great topping for salads, soups, like the Roasted Butternut Squash and Apple Soup with Crisp and Smoky Croutons (page 70), as a coating on our Crispy Baked Onion Rings with Tangy Dipping Sauce (page 52) or as a topping for our Cheesy Cauliflower and Sweet Potato Bake (page 157).

Makes 2½ cups (625 mL)

¼ cup (60 mL) unsalted butter, melted
1 tsp (5 mL) smoked paprika
8 slices of day-old, regular whole wheat bread, cubed
¼ to ½ tsp (1 to 2 mL) sea salt

Preheat the oven to 275°F (140°C). Line a large baking sheet with parchment paper and set aside.

In a small bowl, whisk together the melted butter and paprika. Place the bread cubes in a large bowl, drizzle and toss with the seasoned butter until evenly distributed. Sprinkle with the salt and toss until evenly distributed.

Spread the seasoned cubes on the prepared baking sheet and bake in the oven for 10 minutes. Turn the croutons with a spatula and bake for another 10 minutes. Check the croutons for crispness and bake for another 5 minutes or until crisp and golden. Store for up to 2 weeks in a resealable container at room temperature.

DAIRY-FREE OPTION Replace the butter with grapeseed oil.

GLUTEN-FREE OPTION Replace the whole wheat bread with gluten-free bread.

VEGAN OPTION Replace the butter with grapeseed oil.

SOURDOUGH STARTER

Make your own sourdough starter and then our Homemade Sourdough Noodles (see page 178). Eat up the benefits of fermented food and know what ingredients you're cooking with. It is truly this easy!

Makes 2 cups (500 mL)

1 cup (250 mL) warm water
1 tsp (5 mL) active dry yeast
1 cup (250 mL) all-purpose flour
Pinch of sugar

Place the warm water into a 4-cup (1 L) mason jar and sprinkle the yeast on top. Cover lightly with a clean kitchen towel and allow to activate for 10 minutes. Stir in the flour. Lightly cover and place on a plate to catch any overflow.

Allow the mixture to sit in a warm place on the counter for 3 to 6 days. The mixture will rise and then reduce as the starter matures. The mixture should have a regular yeast fermentation smell. If distinctive colours, such as pink or orange, appear, they may signify the growth of harmful bacteria, so discard and start over.

After the mixture has risen and reduced, cover and refrigerate until ready to use. Stir before use. Always keep 1 cup (250 mL) of starter in the container. Once you have removed some starter for use, replace it with equal parts flour and water and a large pinch of sugar to feed the fermentation. Allow the starter to sit on the counter until bubbly again. (For example, if you remove ½ cup (125 mL) of starter, you would stir in ¼ cup (60 mL) of flour, ¼ cup (60 mL) of warm water and a large pinch of sugar.) Sourdough starter never expires if it's fed once a week and always kept in the refrigerator.

ACKNOWLEDGEMENTS

Loving thanks to our husbands who inspire and critique us daily: Ian Green and Paul Hemming, and to our super-amazing daughters, Sydney, Alyssa and Aston.

We are grateful for the support of Vera Friesen, Darryl Amey and Bill and Val Green, the extended Green family, John and Beryl Barber, Gary and Karen Barber, John, Heather and Ella Barber, David and Sue, and Sam and Baylea Barber.

We will forever be grateful to those who continue to inspire us but have passed, our beloved dad, Swen Runkvist, Ray and Joy Hemming and our hardworking, persevering grandparents. We appreciate the inspiration, support and love from our wonderful extended family, the Runkvists, the Arps, the Deasons, and all of our family in Norway. How on earth did we get so lucky?

We are so grateful to our numerous industry advisors and supporters who answer our questions without fail and continue to engage us, support and actively promote our books across the globe: Sergio and Lisa Nuñez de Arco, Marcos and Alex Guevara and everyone at Andean Naturals, our favourite food scientists; Laurie Scanlin and Claire Burnett, Bob Moore and everyone at Bob's Red Mill, Edouard Rollet, Mathieu Senard and Antoine Ambert and every single rock star at Alter Eco, Jeffrey and Amy Barnes at Edison Grainery, our Peruvian friends, Francisco Diez-Canseco and Magdalena Diez-Canseco, and that fabulous food guy George Aramayo down under in Australia! Much thanks to our publishing director Andrea Magyar, publicist Trish Bunnett, our tireless editor Rachel Brown and the whole Penguin Random House team!

We also thank all of our dear friends for the inspiration and continued encouragement, for recipe testing and just being so unconditionally cool: Sara Busby, Kerri Rosenbaum Barr, Sandi Blydo, Sandi Wasylyniuk, Charlene Drozd, Michelle Klassen, Bridget and Stephen Halfyard, Mia and Ian and the Kruger Family, Tara and Jake Trottier, our super-fab food stylist Nancy Midwicki, our expert big-league photographer Ryan Szulc (and all-star style-expert, Madeleine Johari!), Robert McCullough, Ken and Noreen McLean, Sheila, Mark and Jessie Gordon, The Bones: Jamie, Manon, Stevenson and Robin, Jill and Bob Andersen, Craig Billington, the amazing palate of Carolyn Hallett, cooking dynamo Jill Wilcox and her whole superhero team at Jill's Table, Jackie Noble, Harvey and Diane Katz, Joshua Katz, Michelle and Moshe Sigulim, Cheryl Meredith, Ray and Marion Meredith, Sandra and Jeff Field and all of those "Bring It to the Table" gals, David Boan and Allison Walmsley, Marilyn Elliott, Renee Perreira, Guylaine Palmer, Jocelyn Campanaro, super maven Stefani Farkas, Frank Dyson, Rose Gage and Eddy Smith, Elizabeth "Lily" Smith, Linda Beaudoin, Theresa Nesbitt, Colin and Amanda Gillan, Michele Lawrence,

Gordon Kirke, The Addersons, Shela Shapiro, Heather Dyer, Ashley Whitenect, Ken and Mary Kruger, Keith Marnoch, Robert Newton, Roy Johnston, Team Cronin, Terry Paluszkiewicz, Annica Sjoberg, our fab tech-chick Tanya Riemann, and maven pals Susan Thompson in the UK and Conny Mueller in Germany.

To *everyone* in or near our hometown of Saskatoon, Saskatchewan, whether we know you or not, we've seen your pride and support, and it is our honour. Sincerest gratitude!

(photo: Ryan Szulc)

REFERENCES

Atkins, E. 2015. "Canadians eating less meat, taking a bite out of food industry's margins."
    The Globe and Mail. Retrieved November 14, 2015, from www.theglobeandmail.com
    /report-on-business/canadians-eating-less-meat-taking-a-bite-out-of-food-industrys-margins
    /article26373758/.

Chilkov, N. 2012. "The link between grilled foods and cancer." *Huffington Post*.
    Retrieved September 30, 2015, from www.huffingtonpost.com/nalini_chilkov/grilling
    _health_b_1796567.html.

Haspel, T. 2015. "The decline of the red meat industry." *Fortune*. Retrieved November 14, 2015,
    from http: //fortune.com/2015/10/27/red-meat-consumption-decline/.

Pawlick, T. 2006 *The End of Food. How the Food Industry Is Destroying Our Food Supply and
    What You Can Do About It*. pp. 108–119.

Pollan, M. 2006. *The Omnivore's Dilemma: A Natural History of Four Meals*. pp. 208–238, 304–329,
    336–363.

Pollan, M. 2008. *In Defense of Food: An Eater's Manifesto*. pp. 162–169.

Pollan, M. 2013. *Cooked: A Natural History of Transformation*. pp. 58–66.

Rutberg, S. 2015. "Protein to reach nearly $34 billion By 2020." *New Hope Network*.
    Retrieved September 30, 2105, from http://newhope.com/breaking-news
    /protein-reach-nearly-34-billion-2020.

Tencer, D. 2015. "Canadians are eating less beef and pork thanks to rising prices
    and a changing country." *Huffington Post*. Retrieved October 4, 2015,
    from www.huffingtonpost.ca/2015/09/16/canadians-eating-less-meat_n_8147166.html.

INDEX